Dichten =, No. 6

D1714928

Ludwig
Harig

The Trip
to Bordeaux

translated
from the German
by Susan Bernofsky

BURNING DECK, PROVIDENCE 2003

DICHTEN = is a (not quite) annual of current German writing in English translation. Most issues are given to the work of a single author.
Editor: Rosmarie Waldrop.

Individual copies: $10
Subscription for 2 issues: $16
In England: £5.
Subscription for 2 issues: £8. Postage 25p/copy.

Distributors:
Small Press Distribution, 1341 Seventh St., Berkeley, CA 94710
1-800/869-7553; orders@spdbooks.org
Spectacular Diseases, c/o Paul Green, 83b London Rd., Peterborough, Cambs. PE2 9BS, England

for US subscriptions only:
Burning Deck, 71 Elmgrove Ave., Providence RI 02906

The translation of this short novel was made possible by a subsidy from Inter Nationes, Bonn.
Burning Deck is the literature program of Anyart: Contemporary Arts Center, a tax-exempt (501c3), non-profit corporation.

Cover by Keith Waldrop

ISSN 1077-4203
ISBN 1-886224-53-6

THE TRIP TO BORDEAUX

Lastly, continuing to trace from the inside to the outside these states simultaneously juxtaposed in my consciousness, and before reaching the real horizon that enveloped them, I find pleasures of another kind, the pleasure of being comfortably seated

Marcel Proust, *The Way by Swann's*

Bordeaux. A novel that takes place sitting down. A hero who hardly moves, his actions are perspectives, his element trains of thought. The first word creates the situation, concatenations of nouns the atmosphere, continuations follow from the endings of sentences, the plot unfolds in antitheses of thought.

Gottfried Benn, *The Novel of the Phenotype*

CONTENTS

PLACE BIR-HAKEIM

We crossed the Garonne bridge in the twilight and found ourselves at the place de Bir-Hakeim.

Is this the right direction? I asked. Sihdi, I'm worried about your sanity, said Hans. The place de Bir-Hakeim, I said, do I take a right or a left? Petra said: take the one to Bordeaux. We're supposed to turn off at the place de Bir-Hakeim, I said. The map, said Hans, place de Bir-Hakeim. Hadschi Halef Omar Ben Hadschi Abul Abbas Ibn Hadschi Dawuhd al Gossarah!

Bir-Hakeim, said Hans, take a left. Hanno said: keep going straight ahead. Messalina had stopped saying anything at all. I said, but then Hans said: we can also just go straight, and Hanno said: straight ahead or take a left, and I stopped the car, since if we'd kept going straight we'd have wound up driving down the cours Victor Hugo, who said that France was a republic that encompassed all the world, to where it intersects the rue Sainte Catherine, who did not say the human was something to overcome, and then would have followed it south along the edge of the place du général Sarrail, who said something to the effect that in the end victory was the greatest good, past the place de la Victoire onto the cours de la Somme to where it fed into the rue Terrasson, which is where we'd have come from if we'd taken the road to the left and followed the quai des Salinières for a short while, turning off at the rue des Faures, none of whom ever would have said anything like that children are a blessing, and if we had continued on our way past the église St. Michel, the place Canteloup and the tour St. Michel onto rue Gaspard-Philippe, who might have said tomorrow would be a beautiful day, past the place de Maucaillou, across the Clare and past the market halls to the cours de la Marne, which we'd have crossed so as to turn onto the cours de l'Yser and follow it to the place Nansouty, who could never possibly have said Napoleon was what he really was, and if from there we'd driven along the cours de la Somme to where it fed into the rue Terrasson, where we'd never have been if we hadn't taken the cours de la Somme from the place de la Victoire, but rather had followed the cours de l'Argonne and, after a few hundred meters, turned onto the rue Bertrand de Goth, who, if he hadn't been a Frenchman, might almost have said that God is the Good.

So what do we do now, I said. Place de Bir-Hakeim, said Hans, and turned the map upside down. Sihdi, he said, I trust you to make the right choice.

THE FIRST BOTTLE

Go ahead and pour, I said.

Now I'm really curious, said Messalina.

It's got to be at least twenty years old, said Hans.

Are you serious? Hanno said.

Not for me, said Petra.

I said: pour already, and we'll soon enough see.

Messalina said: tastes good.

Hans said: didn't I say so?

Hanno said: it would appear it tastes good to me as well.

Petra said: not for me.

A proper sip, I said, then fan it out on your tongue.

Quite sweet, Messalina said, with a hint of spice.

Believe me, said Hans, Georges' father-in-law forgot to drink this one.

And the finish is so nice, Hanno said, just like oil.

Not to me, Mama, said Petra, just sour.

You shouldn't believe everyone, said Monsieur de Montaigne, because anyone can say anything.

That's why you have to try it, I said, and don't let anyone convince you otherwise.

To me definitely quite sweet, Messalina said, and you shouldn't believe everyone, because not everyone can say everything.

You shouldn't believe everyone, because everyone cannot say everything, Hans said, or is someone claiming that sour is the same as sweet?

So then you shouldn't believe everyone, because not everyone can say not everything, Hanno said.

Not to me, Petra said.

Pour another round, I said.

Quite sweet and a hint of spice, said Messalina.

Do you believe me now that it's at least twenty years old? said Hans.

Nutmeg, said Hanno.

Not for me, said Petra.

I said: quite sweet, but not too sweet.

Messalina said: if it were a bit drier.

Hans said: left to mellow. Maybe Georges' father-in-law just didn't get around to it.

Hanno said: and a finish like oil.

Petra said: but sour.

You're not fanning it out on your tongues, I said, you won't get it that way.

The spice is quite sweet, Messalina said, I'd rather it were a bit drier.

It wouldn't be if Georges' father-in-law hadn't forgotten it, Hans said, but since he did?

All soft in your throat, Hanno said, so oily.

Quite sweet, said Petra, but also sour.

Monsieur de Montaigne thought: you should believe everyone, because anyone can say anything. But he didn't say so.

And so I said: you should believe everyone.

You're right, Messalina said, you should believe everyone, because everyone cannot say everything. And for me it's too sweet.

For you, yes, Hans said, and you can't get beyond that. And consequently you should believe everyone, because everyone cannot say everything.

No, Hanno said, you should believe everyone, because not everyone can say not everything.

13

Petra said: sour-sweet.

Pour us out another round, I said.

The sweetness feels good inside, said Messalina.

It's the years, said Hans.

Now you can get the full taste of it, said Hanno.

Not to me, said Petra.

I said: you have to keep tasting it again and again.

Messalina said: it goes into your fingertips.

Hans said: at this age it has the right bouquet.

Hanno said: we should give it our full attention.

Petra said: but not for me.

Fan it out on your tongues, I said, savor the full bouquet.

I'm drunk, Messalina said, you can go mad on it.

One more drop, Hans said, the last drop does the most good.

One more for me too, said Hanno, we have to get out the very last bit.

What's this, Monsieur de Montaigne thought, whom should we now believe, if anyone can say anything and not everyone can say everything and everyone cannot say everything?

Not for me, Petra said.

CHÂTEAU LALANNE

We had been sitting, we sat, and we would continue to sit until the sun had fallen and we would no longer be sitting as we sat when we had entered this house in order to sit. We had been sitting (not entirely motionless on our four wheels), we sat (standing and lying down, front and back, facing right and left, and with all the furrows of our being), and we would continue to sit, although it (might well agree better with us to go to sleep altogether, rather than continuing to watch over what we are watching). But driving and standing and lying down and sleeping, we sat upon a piece of earth where sitting is sitting and a pleasure (and everything in its place).

There were kitchen chairs, dining room chairs, children's chairs, grandfather chairs, folding chairs, basket chairs, easy chairs, camping stools, deck chairs, rocking chairs, armchairs, wing chairs, wicker chairs, stools, fauteuils. In the bedroom there was a chaise longue, in the parlor a love seat. Around all these chairs there was the house, the veranda, the courtyard and the little garden. There were the walls, the floor, the ceiling, the terrace, the glass roof, the gate with its palings, the garden wall, the lawn, and the sky. What there wasn't were club chairs, leather chairs, Chippendale chairs and a Hollywood swing.

Upon the armchairs lay pillows. These pillows were printed, painted, woven, embroidered. The easy chairs had newspapers draped over their backs, and from the arms of the armchairs dangled shopping bags. Only the grandfather for the grandfather chair was missing, but Petra was the child for the children's chairs. The tomcat Pito perched on one wing of the wing chair, pointing to the sun with his right rear paw and licking his backside.

The days passed, and we moved from the chaise longue in the bedroom to the armchairs in the parlor, from the armchairs in the parlor to the chairs on the veranda, from the chairs on the veranda to the garden stools. Day after day passed, and we moved with the sun.

We moved to the armchairs and straight chairs of the parlor. There were dining room chairs that were covered in chintz and dated from the era when Monsieur Desgranges, great-grandfather of the notaire, had swapped glass beads for Senegalese and, in their place, brought home a shipload of rum from Guadeloupe; there were basket chairs in which Georges' father-in-law had sat, forgetting that there was still an old bottle of spicy Sauternes in his cellar; there were easy chairs upon which the man with large pores on his nose and cauliflower ears had set his faded cap when he came to shovel out the cesspit; there were camping stools from Ypres and folding chairs from the Monoprix, footstools upon which you could place your shoes while putting them on, and a fauteuil for the aunt from Poitiers. Now we sat upon these chairs and armchairs and shifted their position when the sun moved higher in the sky and entered the rue Lalanne.

There it stood in the south, casting its light into the kitchen. The blue of the plates gleamed, the scales of a fish were glittering, knives and forks cast reflections on the wall. Now the plates were plates and the glasses glasses. The red of the tablecloth was red, and the green of the bottle was green. The legs of the table had edges, the wine jugs had curves, and the dead eyes of the fish were dead.

Beneath the glass roof of the veranda stood a three-legged table. Upon the table stood glasses and a bottle of wine, bread and olives. Around the table stood the chairs upon which we were sitting, two easy chairs for Hanno and Messalina, a basket chair for Hans, a dining room chair covered in chintz for me, and a child's chair with two pillows for Petra. We sat on the chairs with the glasses and wine in front of us, the bread and the olives. We sat on the chairs, eating and drinking, and Pito perched on the wing of the wing chair, pointing to the sun with his right rear paw. Sometimes someone would be sitting in the garden beneath the palm tree, or someone might have a seat on the wall beside the gate with its palings, or there would be two people seated on the love seat in the parlor.

Now the armchair pillows were no longer armchair pillows, the books were no longer books, red was no longer red, and even the fruit bowl on the highboy had lost its curve.

Only the chairs were still chairs, even if the kitchen chairs might be dining room chairs, the dining room chairs children's chairs, the children's chairs grandfather chairs, the grandfather chairs folding chairs, the folding chairs basket chairs, the basket chairs easy chairs, the easy chairs camping stools, the camping stools deck chairs, the deck chairs rocking chairs, the rocking chairs armchairs, the armchairs wing chairs, the wing chairs basket chairs, the basket chairs footstools, the footstools fauteuils; and if there was some confusion between the love seat in the parlor and the chaise longue in the bedroom, it wasn't a confusion between things that were there to be sat on, but because one can sit differently upon them, in such a way that sitting is not merely sitting, but also a pleasure (and everything in its place).

only   the athletic nature of the Southern Europeans
the characteristic features of the woods
the rendezvous in a certain region
the light surrounding my window
his urgency in coming and going
the thought born in conversation

because the athletic nature of the woods
the characteristic features in a certain region
the rendezvous surrounding my window
the light in coming and going
his urgency in conversation
the thought born of the Southern Europeans

but   the athletic nature in a certain region
the characteristic features surrounding my window
the rendezvous in coming and going
the light in conversation
his urgency of the Southern Europeans
the thought born of the woods

and   the athletic nature surrounding my window
the characteristic features in coming and going
the rendezvous in conversation
the light of the Southern Europeans
his urgency of the woods
what is born in a certain region

or   the athletic nature in coming and going
the characteristic features in conversation
the rendezvous of the Southern Europeans
the light of the woods
his urgency in a certain region
what is born surrounding my window

even   the athletic nature in conversation
the characteristic features of the Southern Europeans
the rendezvous of the woods
the light in a certain region
his urgency surrounding my window
what is born in coming and going

possible

THE HURLY-BURLY

Once matters had begun in the accustomed manner, the company clearly and at once saw that our preparing to rouse ourselves was wasted effort, for commonly when we had set our minds to rousing ourselves in the accustomed manner, what ensued thereon was the near immediate conclusion of the said rousing, notwithstanding whatever effort we might give ourselves. An attempt beforehand at rousing ourselves had already resulted in the said rousing's near immediate end, as commonly ensues in the accustomed manner following the attempt at rousing. It matters little by what means this be attempted, the elusive nature of the goal being already certain. Several days afterwards as again we undertook to rouse ourselves, Hans addressed the company thus: You may remember to have witnessed the outcome of our last undertaken rousing. Yet did we not heed these sage words, but again undertook to rouse ourselves, with the near immediate conclusion in the accustomed manner following the attempt at rousing.

The beginning of it was in Hans asking the child: has the puss had his milk? and the child replying: Forsooth, he has not! and Hans saying thereupon: matters being such, we had best remain at home. Whereupon saith the child: Mother hath not yet packed her medicaments, and saith the Mother: Lukkel, hast thou the keys, and I said: where in the devil's name is my wife, and Hans said: indeed, I have need of a visit there myself.

If the child had given the puss his milk and if Hanno had packed her medicaments, and if I had had the keys, and if my wife had descended from the place where Hans averred she was, we had presently been prepared to depart.

But the child had been neglectful, and Hanno's medicaments were packed in another of her bags, and I knew not where were the keys, and my wife was not to be seen, and Hans also had need of a visit to where he thought her to be, and if she really had been where Hans thought her to be and if she really came out from where Hans thought her to be, Hans had still been unable to repair thither, he having said: matters being such, we had best remain at home.

But all of us expecting she should emerge presently, we hastened our preparations and the child hied her into the kitchen and fetched a dish for the puss's milk, and Hanno came running into the room and began digging in her bags in search of her medicaments, and I betook myself within and began sifting amongst my chaffer to lay my hands on the keys, Hans continually braying whether my wife were not soon to descend from where he thought her to be and muttering without respite thus: matters being such, we had best remain at home.

But then had the child already issued out of the kitchen carrying the dish of milk. But the puss having had his milk, Hanno still had not her medicaments, and when Hanno suddenly came running out having found her medicaments amongst her bags, I still had not found the keys, the idea having suddenly come to me that I had not put them amongst my chaffer after all, and so withdrew and searched about my jerkin and when I had found them and intending to go back out again I am caught on the leg of a chair and let fall the keys and Hans stumbleth upon the dish of milk and the milk runneth the length of the floor.

And thus in a trice the puss had milk no more and I had keys no more and herewith began the child to howl and weep and Hanno fetched out her medicaments and swallowed down a dose of pills speaking thus: I am not well at ease. Hans took up the puss's dish and I took up the keys and still my wife was not to be seen.

If the child had at once given the puss his milk and Hanno had put her medicaments properly amongst her bags and I had had the keys at hand and my wife had descended from the place where Hans thought her to be, then were the child not obliged to hie herself to the kitchen to fetch the puss his milk and Hanno had not been obliged to betake herself to the other room in search of her medicaments and I had not gone a-hunting amongst my chaffer for the keys and the devil knoweth how to excuse my absent wife.

As we have showed you before, once matters had begun in the accustomed manner, the company clearly and at once saw that our preparing to rouse ourselves was wasted effort, for commonly when we had set our minds to rousing ourselves in the accustomed manner, what ensued thereon was the near immediate conclusion of the said rousing, notwithstanding whatever effort we might give ourselves. An attempt beforehand at rousing ourselves had already resulted in the said rousing's near immediate end, as commonly ensues in the accustomed manner following the attempt at rousing. It matters little by what means this be attempted, the elusive nature of the goal being already certain. Several days afterwards as again we undertook to rouse ourselves, Hans addressed the company thus: You may remember to have witnessed the outcome of our last undertaken rousing. Yet did we not heed these sage words, but again undertook to rouse ourselves, with the near immediate conclusion in the accustomed manner following the attempt at rousing.

For all at once the door to the chamber springeth open and whom do I behold issuing therefrom but my wife. Let us depart, saith she, but then saith Hans, who had expected that she would issue from a door other than the door to the chamber, he having also need of a visit to where he thought her to be, and had she descended from where he thought her to be, still had Hans been unable to repair thither, he having said: matters being such, we had best remain at home, saith Hans, as we have showed you before: now we had verily best remain at home.

THE PRELIMINARIES OF M. DE MONTAIGNE

My chapter headings were not released into the world by the indeterminacy of the word hoc in the theory of trans-substantiation. These anecdotes and the many quotes contained in them are not always plain examples and do not always exhaust their subject matter, much as in the case of a man who, needing fire, visits his neighbor to obtain some. I sometimes lose my thread, if not the laprobe. I prefer the sort of gait familiar in poetry, with unexpected leaps, whether it be on horseback, at table or in bed, either since I myself am one person one day, another on another, front and back, facing left and right, and in all my natural attitudes, but especially on horseback, where I engage in my most protracted conversations. And when he has arrived at the home of his neighbor, where a large splendid fire is burning, he takes a seat. But more because I enjoy being in the company of a dog we know. Among the Basques and other foreign peoples, we experience just the same thing, provided it is not Latin. I am in the habit of taking a seat on such occasions. My trains of thought bear upon one another as it is with a man whose language we do not understand. I present myself standing and lying down. Where the responsibility lies has not yet been established. Those of different nations do not regard one another as human, and the one warming himself forgets forthwith his intention to obtain fire for his own home.

I am presenting here an entire palette of anecdotes, and with all the furrows of my being. May the reader not devote his full attention to my matter alone, just as there is no better way of judging a horse's strength than by pulling him up short and sharp. It is, for those possessed of a sound memory, always difficult that we do not understand each other. If it were the same thing to grasp hold of a book and grasp its contents, he could make infinitely many essays out of it so as to preserve them in his memory that we might fail to understand them. Lying is indeed an accursed vice, I do it so as to have a weapon in my grasp for use against will-o-the-wisp premature criticisms, for we understand them no better than do they us, precisely in order that they no longer the more.

These here are my personal turns of phrase and these are aphorisms, ever more with such quotations of imprecise and on occasion contradictory notions, points of view, comparisons or justifications. I am incautiously and with considerable noise pursuing a beast of a different sort. The inattentive reader will lose his way, but not I. A word is always entering the picture in some way obscured, though at times aslant. My activity consists of notating the course of diverse happenstance and constantly changing phenomena. I clutch. I have the courage. I can discern in them. I leave to others to point out. I incriminate. It pleases me nonetheless. Not only the point of view. But rather to that of my. But rather of nothing other than. But rather to the structure of my quotes. But rather to their in this sense. And thus I can with certainty only to the extent to which formerly under different illumination. When I am the least in search of them. When I am unable instantly to pin them down. When in my isolated. When each time with a single piece. To those whose aspect pleases me not as because failing to notice.

Perhaps I will one day learn something of external reality. And then. And that. And with them. Or did once know something of it. The most profound and foolish. The ones that cause me the most. The idea that ceaselessly. The objects among other. That give to my representations more even than. That I in my. Most of them often a for me. The human. As I do betwixt these self-discovered.

How instantly my knowledge of these, being subjected to new interpretation, takes on unforeseen nuances. The end of his story only through the word. The knowledge of the outer world which brings me to my. Which I do not thus. Not so much from me as from my. To speak and only through the word. Through which the most essential matter entering my pasture and how much more to consign to speech. To look upon and see it. As it begins it. It cannot surprise us that. And for others vexed by silence. Which would render it unnecessary from whom they have been taken. For this reason they can just as well regard us dumb animals as we do them.

Venturing beyond my topic to ideas and speech as original meaning. Sometimes their to these only by a sort of stamp. Arrive suddenly. Spend ignorant. Remain uncovered. Retain nothing. Make. Describe. Testify. Judge. Locate. From this borrowed my notion to point more decisively and clearly to linguistic misunderstandings as of all other that. But sometimes intentionally something containing beneath their. Hinted at. Full on. Concentrated. Foreign matter, borrowings is property to the reproach from. My representations there in particular not further in my. In connection with respect precisely to. I embrace our language, transplant and set. Be it that my something in books here. Taken that they are to further positions.

A Church Father says, even if on earth there be. Community by means of untrue. Misunderstandings such as fateful. Not properly understood to human. Diverting mass has weaknesses and error. That we are aided by. Our standing here together just as little as like many and thus.

It not being my principal goal to emphasize or elaborate. And so not giving my and thus for. For here I must note that. Concluding my book and how many others can by its presentation often. Responding to recommendations will we express and bolder thoughts will lightly. The correct selection emerging. Whether I by my and through this toward me. Should proclivity not appearing pleases what to me that. He shall. And for use as long as the momentum. This I might have. They stand as if in place of. For in such case I can even. Classify, reshape them. Who wanted to rake through them more thoroughly, instantly their disappearance. Had wanted. Have its effect on me: Had gone. Naturally. To these things suffice. Circumstances or. Nonetheless giving my characteristic quarrels. I want.

Everything published by contemporary writers, especially young ones, shall be ripped to shreds.

THE MUMMIES

The old man raised his stick and brought it down on a mummy. There was a sound like someone whacking a papier-mâché head at carnival. He said: this is General von Preissac, he was killed in a duel with M. de la Chalotais. The old man thrust his stick through the hole left by the dagger. When he withdrew it, it smelled of sheepskin.

In the crypt of Mont-Michel, the mummies are chained to the wall. There is a wooden balustrade in front of them, and the old man said: défense de toucher. The mummies just stand there, clasping one another's hands. They have been frozen in a ronde macabre, their eye sockets gaping, mouths stretched in a yawn.

The old man said: here you see the bearer of burdens. He made a wager that he could carry two thousand five hundred pounds. But this inhuman exertion caused his muscles to burst. He swung his stick and struck the bearer's right shoulder. Voyez, he said, this shoulder carried two thousand five hundred pounds, but the weight of it finished him off.

The old man took a few steps and said: here you see the family that fell victim to mushroom poisoning. The father, the mother, the boy, the girl. And each time he struck at the leather dolls with his stick. Upon the faces of these unhappy creatures, you can still read the traces of their agony, he said. But the faces didn't look any different from all the others.

The old man pulled out a blue-and-white checked handkerchief and blew his nose with it. He waved it around in the air, then stuffed it back in his pocket. There are no bacilli in the vault, he said, everything dried up seven hundred years ago. Only the skin and the bones were preserved beneath the sand.

He took a few more steps. These two women died of cancer, he said, poking around in the hollows of their breasts. Messalina had the hiccups. (I came into the world with all my organs sound, and almost perfect. My digestion is excellent.) All I could smell was the sheepskin. It made me think of a cobbler's workshop.

The old man put his hand in the outer left-hand pocket of his coat and produced a tin. This is Pater Félix, he said, lifting up a scrap of cloth with his stick. This is a piece of his soutane, he said. He was the confessor of Saint-Michel. The old man dropped the bit of cloth and clamped the stick between his legs. Holding the tin firmly in his left hand, he removed the lid with the fingers of his right and wedged it between the tin and his left palm.

Behold the Negress, he said, we call her the Odalisque. His stick was still clamped between his legs. The Odalisque, he said, no one knows how she got here.

The old man inserted his right thumb and index finger into the tin and brought something to his right nostril. At the same time as he was blocking off his left nostril with his middle finger, he inhaled energetically through his right nostril, which he instantly released.

And here is a small boy who was buried alive, he said. The mummy of the child was curled into a ball. The child's head was

29

thrown back. His fingernails were buried in the hollows of his palms. His bent knees were once the lever for the force that would have been needed to burst open his grave. His throat is still swollen with the cries he uttered. The old man opened his mouth and sneezed.

He said: look at the eye of this man here, it has been perfectly preserved. We gazed at the eye. It was staring blankly out of its seven-hundred-year-old face. And was no Tutankhamen in the Valley of Kings at Luxor, one that was nowhere recorded but was simply there, neither celebrated nor avenged, simply there with the eye of no longer what laughs and sheds tears but is merely reminiscent of eye, of something like glass that has decayed, something like stone that shatters in splinters on the floor, something like pebble faded decayed splintered shattered in a hammock of flesh and bone fastened to shreds in its socket, the cords severed, blind pebble in a setting of stone, hanging shrivelled in slack moorings, the eye faded the iris in the sands of the millennium, pupil decayed, cones and rods shattered, splintered what of glass and living matter, faded, decayed, shattered, splintered, and the retina torn, abraded, transmitting not a single glance.

Voyez, the old man said, guiding his stick to one of the shrivelled heads. A man who wore a wig. He moved his stick across the top of the right ear and lifted up the wig with its point. And here a mother with babe in arm, the old man said. Voyez, the child still has a tooth. He leaned over the balustrade, indicating the tooth with his index finger. Dante wrote nothing more moving, he said.

The hunchback, he now cried out, behold the hunchback! Un bossu, he cried, par-devant et par-derrière. Un drôle de momie, he said and laughed, bringing his stick down upon the leather protuberance, struck and laughed and said: deux nouveaux francs pour cette danse macabre! and laughed and brought his stick down on the hump.

THE BAR

There's no mistaking the signs of genuine Teutonic thirst when it comes to beer. We were able to procure some just around the corner. We stood at the bar for a bit to catch the sports news. The bartender had switched to another channel. But we were well-versed in the General's techniques of obstacle avoidance.

The fat bartender was keeping busy with his bottles. He poured out the green sixteenth-of-a-liter shots for the Bordelais to just below the mark. Then he picked up the siphon bottle and pressed the lever until soda fizzed into the glasses. But the sixteenths-of-a-liter were only eighteenths, and after the second glass the men had imbibed not two sixteenths but two eighteenths. They stood at the bar, drinking and smoking. The cigarette paper turned black between their lips. Only when they took a sip from their glasses did they remove the cigarettes from their mouths. There were five of them. The first one, who was standing at the far end of the bar, had on corduroy trousers and a blue undershirt. He was standing a bit apart from the others, staring at the shelves of bottles. Now and then he buried his fingers in the luxuriant growth of hair protruding from the neckline of his undershirt. He glanced neither to the left, where the other four were standing, nor to the right, the television screen. But when the other four raised their glasses, he too reached for his glass and drank from it precisely the same quantity as the other four.

Had the drinks been portioned out properly, four glasses at a sixteenth per glass would have brought the men to a grand total of four sixteenths or a quarter liter each, but since the improperly portioned eighteenths resulted in a mere four eighteenths after four glasses, they would have had to consume four and a half eighteenths to reach the quarter-liter mark. Assuming consistent portions throughout, this mark would be reached between the fourth and fifth glasses.

The men stood drinking and smoking, staring and conversing, according to the location and temperament of each. The three standing nearest to the one in the blue undershirt were chatting among themselves. The one in the middle had a red nose with large pores and cauliflower ears. He wore a faded beret and kept saying: c'est mon avis, mon vieux, followed each time by a stroll around the bar. The one standing between him and the one with the blue undershirt had his back turned to the one in the blue undershirt. His cigarette was affixed to the right-hand corner of his mouth. His lips were open, and his upper-jaw prosthesis was hanging loose. He held the thumb and index finger of his left hand pressed against his ear, listening. The conversation was dominated by the third. He stood with his back to me, facing the television. He was discussing the General's technique. The men hoisted their deficient sixteenths and drank.

Had the drinks been portioned out properly, eight glasses at a sixteenth per glass would have brought them to a grand total of eight sixteenths or half a liter each, but since the improperly portioned eighteenths resulted in a mere eight eighteenths after eight glasses, they would have had to consume nine eighteenths to reach the half-liter mark. Assuming equal quantities through-out, this mark would be reached after the ninth glass.

The one standing nearest to the one in the blue undershirt now rattled his loose upper-jaw prosthesis. He said: je crois pas. The one next to the one with the loose false teeth inserted a finger into his left-hand cauliflower ear, said: c'est mon avis, mon vieux, and took his stroll. The one next to the one with cauliflower ears went on tirelessly conversing. He pronounced the General's technique elegant and hence insufficiently forceful. The one next to the one with his back to me was wearing sandals. His feet smelled. He explained to me what he meant when he said the Girodins hadn't quite had the punch to end the season as the French champions. He explained and said: que pensez-vous? Hans didn't smell the smelly feet. But since the one with smelly feet kept saying: que pensez-vous? I kept having to breathe through my nose long enough to answer him. I tried taking shallow breaths, but this made me choke while I was talking, and the man with smelly feet said: à votre santé!

Had the drinks been portioned out properly, twelve glasses at a sixteenth per glass would have brought the men to a grand total of twelve sixteenths or three quarters of a liter each, but since the improperly portioned eighteenths resulted in a mere twelve eighteenths after twelve glasses, they would have had to consume thirteen and a half eighteenths to reach the three-quarter-liter mark. Assuming they continued to drink at a constant rate, this mark would be reached between the thirteenth and fourteenth glasses.

The television was now set to a different channel. But the one with his back to me didn't change his position relative to the screen. He said: the General's politics has a big hole in it. The old man had thrust his stick through the hole in General von Preissac and there had been a smell of sheepskin.

Oh, you're too kind, said Madame Bovary. The one with the corduroy trousers and blue undershirt buried his fingers in his chest hair and gazed at the television for a moment. Dis donc, he said to the bartender, turn it off, won't you? Oh, you know that isn't possible, said Madame Bovary. The bartender said: I have to respect the other guests. The one with the loose upper-jaw prosthesis said to the one with cauliflower ears: je crois pas. The one with cauliflower ears said: c'est mon avis, mon vieux, and set off on his rounds. Madame Bovary said: do sit down, you're making me perfectly ill with your pacing. He returned to the bar, and the men hoisted their glasses once again.

Had the drinks been portioned out properly, sixteen glasses at a sixteenth per glass would have brought them to a grand total of one liter each, but since the improperly portioned eighteenths resulted in a mere sixteen eighteenths after sixteen glasses, they would have had to consume eighteen eighteenths to reach the one liter mark. Assuming they kept at it, this mark would be reached after the eighteenth glass.

A hole, the one with his back to me said to the one with cauliflower ears, the General has driven his cart into the muck and now there's no help for it. If they'd made better use of the outside left, the one with smelly feet said to me, but they didn't, he said, and what does that do for us? Nothing, said Madame Bovary, it's nothing, nothing at all, it's just nerves. I've had enough, said the one with the blue undershirt, turn it off.

Ah, my poor, good piano, said Madame Bovary. Don't you see, the barkeeper said, I can't with all the guests here. Yes, it's just, I hardly know myself, said Madame Bovary. Je crois pas, said the one with loose false teeth. The men brought their glasses to their lips and drank.

Had the drinks been portioned out properly, thirty-two glasses at a sixteenth per glass would have brought them to a grand total of thirty-two sixteenths or two liters each, but because of the improperly portioned eighteenths this would be the case only after thirty-six glasses, and so the bartender had saved four glasses per head, which given the difference between a sixteenth and an eighteenth results in a hundred-forty-fourth per glass or four hundred-forty-fourths per four glasses, in other words a thirty-sixth, hence five thirty-sixths per five men, in other words almost one seventh, resulting logically in an improper gain of one liter per week, which amounts to twelve francs and seventy-five centimes, in a month to fifty-one new francs, in a year to six hundred and twelve, in ten years to six thousand one hundred and twenty francs, which is enough for a new Peugeot quatre-cent-trois complete with radio and seat covers, assuming the General lives to see his eighty-first birthday and keeps the outside left in reserve.

C'est mon avis, mon vieux, said the one with cauliflower ears and set off on another trip around the bar. Madame Bovary took a sip of water and turned her face to the wall. I am thirsty; oh! so thirsty! she said. The men hoisted their glasses and drank. Madame Bovary was seized by an attack of nausea so sudden that she scarcely had time to retrieve her handkerchief from under the pillow. The endomorph whose character was full of holes kept refilling the men's glasses. They drank and gossiped and, at the very moment Madame Bovary breathed her last, the barkeeper worked the lever of the siphon bottle with oblivious calm.

TABLE TALK

O Hans be loose and plucke the goose, don't gulch all the juice,
but give a poor student a bite of the caboose

                      between the sort
you have before partaking of anything at all and the sort that
follows upon the second and third courses of a meal

                              of all
manner of smoked and dryed and salted and raw meat: further
many barrels full of rank dog-befarted boar's flesh, of farced
fatted beeves, wethers, emasculated bullocks, gelded calves'
chalderns, miscarven oxen from vicar or knacker, gallant salligots
with garlick, mouflin mouflard, fat cocklicranes neatly trussed,
rams' heads and sheep's pluck, brisk brisket, ballocksed lamb
collops, sheats with bristles intacter, bacon with bristles excoriater,
flesh of sows and hogs' haslets with mustard: and a good supply
of heavy bum cuts of cur and coxcomb, all larded with the onion
of the Egyptian gods, stuffed, stewed, soured in vinegar and
sour-vinegar-soused

                    as we on some occasions pave the stomach
without art and on others whet and tickle the palate

                              without
regard to the everlasting quarrel between the Arab and the
Galenist whether it be moister or drier if roasted or stewed

whereas the Germans are almost
equally pleased to imbibe all manner of vegetation, being more
intent on moistening their throats than on the savor
further
down in the text: tripe in brine
they washed their arse-guts with
a sponge
for the killing of a pig is among slaughters the most
merry aside from church-vermin with inherited riches and
widows who play at the close buttock game with might and
main
for I consider it more barbarous to eat a man alive than
to eat him dead; to tear by rack and torture a body still full of
feeling, to roast it by degrees, and then give it to be trampled
and eaten by dogs and swine
lusty as sheep-shearing time at
Nabal's
they roast him, eat him all together, and send portions
to their absent friends
for which cause if we should foresee
what foul Liberties these Cannibalistic Man-gulchers would
belabour upon us when kilt
a practice which we have not
only read about but seen within recent memory, not between
ancient enemies, but between neighbors and fellow-citizens
and
willingly though a man might suffer himself to be spitted for it
is sayed a succulent platter be worth putting one's head in a
noose for
it requires more time and persistance on the scholar's
part
so eate drinke & be merry
as the saying goes

Things would never have come about the way they came about upon the casemates of Blaye if things had come about the way Georges had wanted to make them come about, assuming it to have been in his power to make them come about in the way he wanted to have them come about. He was, however, unable to make them come about the way he wanted them to come about, since, after all, wanting and being able are two different things if one wants to have something come about that one is unable to cause to come about. Someone who wants to will be able to be able, provided it lies in his power to be able to do the thing he wants, but someone who wants to be able to do what he wants to be able to do because he wants to be able to do it may experience something like what was experienced by Georges, who had wanted to have things come about in a way he had been unable to make them come about, because it hadn't been in his power to be able to cause them to come about the way he had wanted to have them come about.

Georges may very well have wanted to have a sunset appear above the Gironde because he is a good person and wanted to have a sunset appear for us such as we had never before seen, but he was unable to be able to make one appear, and thus he was in fact unable to make one appear. There was a cloud in the way, and there's nothing one can do about clouds, particularly where sunsets are concerned. And so things did not come about in quite the way they were supposed to, despite Georges' wanting so badly for them to come about in just this way.

But the sunset, too, was unable to want and thus also unable to be able, it was no use our having taken up such a favorable position upon the western bastion of the citadel. The Gironde lay directly in front us, the broad arm of the river and the strip of land on its opposite shore, and if things had come about the way Georges had wanted to have them come about, we would have seen the setting sun just to the right of the pointed strip of land above the horizon of the lake, because we had calculated that this edge of the polygon, which featured a slight inward curve such that the depth of the curve constituted no more than one-sixth of the length of the line connecting the two corners of the bastion, offered the clearest view.

That which the edge of the polygon permitted us was denied us by the cloud. It had entered from the south-west, at first nothing more than an insignificant bit of haze which began to thicken above the Médoc and was developing into a cumulus by the time it reached the pointed strip of land on the opposite shore. Then it mounted up quickly, swelling to form an unwieldy mass. Its outlines began to fray, to disperse, and at its center the sky flashed briefly into view. The Arcimboldi head acquired a long nose, and Messalina said: it wasn't meant to be.

Georges had wanted to have things come about in a certain way because he wanted them to and therefore was in a position to want without being able to be able. He had wanted his wanting to suffice, but when he was supposed to be able, the cloud appeared. He was no longer able to be supposed to be able, but how is a person supposed to be supposed to be able when he wants to be supposed to and a cloud is present?

And so things had come about in a way they weren't supposed to, although Georges had wanted to have them come about differently, but he had been unable to make them come about the way he wanted because it hadn't been in his power to be able to make them come about the way he wanted to be able to have them come about. The cloud was now no longer a head, it had ceased to be anything more than a simple cloud above a strip of land. Similarly, the sunset wasn't a sunset at all, and the position we had taken up upon the curtain wall between the bastions of the citadel wasn't a position with the clearest view of a sunset but rather a completely ordinary position overlooking ramparts and ditches.

Being supposed to be able to want was certainly within Georges' power, since after all he's a good person, but being able to be supposed to want (what do I know?) isn't something one can just perform on command, being supposed to want to be able is for the virtuous, but Georges?, and wanting to be supposed to be able, splendid, but we had that with Schiller already, which leaves us with being able to want to be supposed to, a likely story, and wanting to be able to be supposed to, not a shred of hope, because of the cloud.

THE CITADEL

A stone's throw from the curtain wall lay the remains of the tenaille. In another age, it had served the purpose of shielding the sally port that was set into the enceinte, allowing a greater portion of the ditch to be raked with fire and providing a sector within the ditch where soldiers could gather to prepare for sorties against attackers attempting to breach the ditch.

Petra sat at the exit to the sally port. Crouching upon the remains of the tenaille, she gathered her thoughts and then raked the ditch. As her salvos whizzed over the ditch's edge, her face took on the tranquil expression of a gunner beginning to feel his magazine unloading automatically.

The outer wall of the main ditch, which was part dry, part wet, did not run parallel to the faces of the bastion but rather grew narrower as it approached the bastion's point. This had the advantage of making it possible for a superior number of gunners to oppose an enemy counterbattery on the glacis, since thanks to this construction the flank was longer than the stretch of glacis directly opposite.

Petra's magazine was unloading automatically, part dry, part wet. The bullets, which grew narrower near the tip, exited from the magazine at regular intervals. They whizzed above the tenaille and exploded at the edge of the ditch. Some of the shots were direct hits, some ricocheted.

The ditch extended far in front of the curtain wall to accommodate a large ravelin that had been built there, a sort of outwork with shoulders which also held a small keep. A trench branching off from the dry ditches provided drainage.

The direct hits and ricochets exited from Petra's magazine. Now she had found her rhythm and fixed her thoughts on the task at hand. She gave it her all. The magazine spat out the salvos, the artillery attacked from the flanks, the ravelin shook beneath the bursts of fire. Sweat broke out, but Petra diverted the water into the trench.

An uncovered walkway ran diagonally across the bottom of the ditch. An extension of the recessed passageway cutting across both enceinte and tenaille, it linked the sections of the fortification divided by the ditch. This walkway was separated from the ditch proper by glacis-like embankments.

Petra's water was flowing through the ditch. Following the turns and hollows of the ditch bed, it went in search of low-lying terrain. The rivulet washed against the mounds of earth and moistened the hard-packed soil of the ditch bottom. The salvos were still raking the wall of the ditch. Inner composure and resolution continued to determine the regularity of the salvos.

The double caponiere had the additional function of eliminating the blind spot that developed when one was firing from the high rampart and thus of complementing the low-angle raking of the ditch.

Petra noticed the blind spot and switched to low-raking the ditch. Obeying an inner compulsion, she worked her magazine to get out the last bit. She was now almost entirely depleted.

Inner composure and inner compulsion, resolution and submission to an inexorable necessity had consumed her strength. The cartridges were exiting from the magazine more sparingly now, only thin-walled casings tumbled into the ditch.

The double caponiere was reproduced at the two shoulder points of the ravelin in the form of single caponieres which performed the same functions as the double caponiere with respect to the ravelin's faces.

But Petra's capacities had now come to an end. Feebly she squeezed out her last few cartridges, and then her magazine was empty. Hanno and Messalina leapt across the ditch and took cover. They readied their magazines, but no salvos were heard. You've got to shoot! Petra cried, I've run out. But Hanno and Messalina appeared to be chronically jammed. Desperately they struggled to get off even a single shot. They had taken aim with their magazines in position, but the ditch remained unrazed.

To prevent these caponieres from interrupting the link between the various fronts of the ditch, however, they were separated from the adjoining sections of the fortification by broken ambulatories on their wings.

Hanno and Messalina pulled their triggers. Sweat broke out on their foreheads and flowed into the trench. They flailed their arms about. The white flags appeared behind the ditch and fluttered in the light breeze. Now Hans and I intervened in the battle.

The covered walkway was rigged out with firing positions that took on the character of sectors since they were separated from the long branches of the covered walkway by defensible traverses with ambulatories.

Hans leapt onto the outer traverse and covered my position. From the inner traverse, I got off a few ricochet shots. The ricocheting bullets enfiladed the stone, the salvos bounced off the side extensions and crashed into the traverse. Hans opened rolling fire from the outer traverse. The grenades clattered through the ditches, caponiere and sally port resounded with the thunder of gunshot, powder smoke filled the air above the traverse. Petra dashed across the ditch, Messalina took down the white flag, and Hanno cried: Gaaas!

General von Preissac now appeared upon the casemate with the hole in his chest. Use the outside left, he shouted, and the ditch filled with the smell of sheepskin.

THE SELF-PORTRAIT OF
M. DE MONTAIGNE

I have made my book to no greater extent than it has made me. So I can be recognized by the unrecognizability of nothing the whole. The broad and domed brow. The clear and soft eye. The small ears and mouth. The well-shaped head. The fresh complexion. The pleasing face. The odourless body. I enjoy it doubly when it is touched by the wind of chance. There moves now and then within me. When I dance, I dance. My thinking moves not only forward. I taste myself. When I sleep, I sleep. Depending how I twist and contort my limbs. But when the man is too small there's no help for it.

I roll myself up into a ball. I am well fit for this. I can do nothing but speak. I find it admissible and pleasant. I prepare myself for it. I am eager for it. I am satisfied with it. I scrutinize myself from close at hand. I have never quite managed to. I make the serviette rather dirty. I attempt. I throw myself so greedily upon it. I also take pleasure in the company of beautiful women. I myself am the King of Matter. I do not decay. I cannot distinguish one sort of grain from another. All this taken together does not yet suffice to produce a handsome man.

It hovers, it floats. But not lacking in physical charms. But one must. In the daytime I can. I can between meals. I can with perspiration-drenched. To quench my thirst I can. I cannot for very long bareheaded. I can before lying down to sleep at night. I could even without a tablecloth. But I cannot have my hair cut after dinner. And yet I am not of the opinion that I have hereby defined myself exhaustively. Other kinds of beauty are for the women.

The wisdom that pleases me has no memory. In the case of everyday friendships I would have just as much difficulty as without my shirt. Priceless, singular ones I have often full of joy. Those whom I find pleasing, who move with exuberance when they speak or without canopy and curtains for my bed. Who with living matter and reality until a long time after supper not pure water or standing. Bearing, expression, voice, attire. Beauty of stature is the sole masculine beauty, you silly ape. All these things I observe within myself. Without marveling. More than the Germans or Italians. The others do not see us.

Go to bed. Sleep. Fornicate. Not keeping one's clothes on. Without my gloves. After meals and in the morning, while getting up. To drink pure wine. White serviette. Not to breakfast early in the morning. Garden at table. Not to wash. Taking pleasure in the world. With great reluctance in the German manner. Of spoon and fork I make little use. They have only a vague inkling. They do not see us so very. Religion has gotten tangled up on their tongues. The abstinence of Cistercians and Capuchins when one has dealings with them. This awkward composite condition. One could rather have them bite into hot iron. To show myself to them I wouldn't have any sense.

That physicality has a strong hold on me. The fact that women also. Daily, hourly I might fancy. But rather the senses of sight and touch during love. Tantalizing with the goal of. Charming without intellectual charms but with physical. Hungry. Without abstaining from sensual and temporal pasture. When I am walking by myself in a beautiful orchard, even if my thoughts dwell for part of the time on distant events, I bring them back for another part to the walk. To the orchard to the. Pleasure. Languidly and without tedium. Light-hearted and affable. Natural. Upstanding. Outright. Complete. Always. Warm. Fairly cold inside only when I am dead. Mankind. Friendships. Solitude. Inspiration. Activity. Joys. Deeds. Gestures. Facial expressions. Inclinations. Writing. Trials. Thoughts. Idleness. Openness. Consideration. Order. Whim. Progress. No marvels. Bitter, harsh morality is not to my liking. My little ship moves over the water when all its sails are set.

From the best side my objective. Somewhat chary especially when as. All repulsive affectations suspicious. Neither the desire to build nor hunting nor tending the garden. Neither out-of-doors nor in the barn. My intentions just as the wind wiser than we. To say everything I dare to undertake. To my wishes things can recommend outer appearance. My favorite qualities perfectly open and devoid of. Unpolished, just as they come to me. Even in my words as simple as if I'd said. When in my country someone means to say a person lacks all understanding, he says: it is still our own bottom that we sit upon. As for the rest in more refined matters to contradict as needed. As for the rest always.

Thus I draw conclusions and make admissions. To my own. Not to those of others. That is a much rarer matter, much more difficult, but without renunciation. Still we must desist from. Who during my lifetime. Which during my lifetime. Everything is with my. Losing it would still on the whole not only in reality but. Just as we are recognize myself to. We are nothing for. But rather as we to ourselves. Only and and in order and or is. And the decent to be experiences but these others are in the. I can still however still. It has grown if one to my own natural. To myself I seem. I am making myself a. Want me as in my. Vivacious in particular when. Myself I cannot. But giving as is in those there is. Ours has no. Is the one whom to spend my. Too long past is still remains. This is perhaps why when I am speaking.

To partake of or only just to have. To do has in addition. One that since it appears to me most definitely and also. Attain the spoken word. And in the process become. Those who are not I cannot to myself. To go and having found it. I still have those who. It is still of relevance since. This latter to myself. Am after all to recognize those. Not every opportunity with. If they are not all too. Having to be would must. Thus I would have if my. To have to myself as my not. To append I seizing upon. In familiar and to the. He and the others I attributed much. Better known of course makes one. Having to be thus to become. To approach them and to attain that. Yet to fill up and to preserve. Then that I am not easily able to fail in. For if in my eyes one of the two, I find those who with my and that to them. Affect one coming to oneself. As for example my chattering. Giving oneself over. To give. To give up.

More of a hindrance than in regret. Since it can be lost not because burdensome. This entire manner is because of men such as me. Which are part of life. That's what one believes one believes. If I now complain of this, then for the reason that I am able to note that the others would have to be thus without the intellectual. Primarily spirit having comported themselves with such outward peace as worth in their isolation for lack of. For really to speak to oneself in the usual madcap as though one despised the pain. Making a thing valuable is nothing. And not according to their contents. Contempt for life set against my own contempt. From our ailments a solid foundation in a melancholy. Contempt for life the most horrible.

Great power of which I am treating I must relate. Particularly striking are opinions on stilts. One ought to not but keeping. With much less attention the one most emphatically demanded. Why does time present itself with exaggeration? That when in pain one should pull oneself together. To be half where we are already so very much. Not I. To rail against when it causes pain.

As for myself, I am enamored of life. Dancing, laughing, selling, paying up, loving, hating, chatting with loved ones and treating oneself in a benevolent, just manner, not giving in, not giving oneself the lie, carving properly, observing oneself secretly at close range, walking upon our legs, mounting on stilts, eating for perhaps three hours upon the most exalted throne in the world, but without greens and salad. And the wind loves to roar and surge. There's nothing we desire of our own free will, as if these were all quite necessary items. Tears move me to tears, even crocodile and painted tears.

My plan is open to attack. One must admit. I owe no one an accounting. With this opinion against me. To relate less about oneself than one is inclined, this is folly and not by any means modesty. Vainglory is founded upon renunciation. And the most fearsome of our illnesses, contempt for oneself. I am an honest man. Learning and practical wisdom nothing, but the ability to take stock. My shame: since I have been accustomed to this since childhood, I allow myself for want of a better example to be seduced into overeating. And what happened to me just last month: it became apparent that I did not know what was the role of sourdough in baking bread. I am also unable to keep straight the various sorts of distinctions. I often dream that I am dreaming, without the least exertion. But I do not know the right way to close a letter.

This makes me particularly attractive. At home in my own private error.

In fine, all this medley that I am scribbling here is but a record of my inner nature.

The turtledoves were flying across the heath.
The sheep were stepping among the loads of hay.
The dung beetle was marching down the dusty road.
The turtledoves were after the dung beetle.
The dung beetle got wind of something.
The sheep were hunting for lupine.
The dung beetle crept into his ball of dung.
The turtledoves landed in the juniper.
The sheep were standing beneath the pines.
The dung beetle was scrabbling.
The sheep were bleating.
The turtledoves were cooing.
The sheep shook their heads.
The turtledoves opened their beaks.
The dung beetle was rolling its dung.
The sheep stepped forward.
The dung beetle marched backward.
The turtledoves flew aboveward.
The grapevine is becoming stunted.
The grapes shrivel.
The sand goes to seed.
It clambers up the pine trees.
It slips into the huts.
It creeps beneath clothes.

The children shovel it into their dolls.
The dogs kick it up against the sheep barn.
The women chew it between their teeth.
The peasants are moving slowly.
The resin drips sluggishly.
The pots fill up gradually.
The sap marks on the trees gape open.
The resin is welling up.
The bark is fragrant.
The peasants are walking on stilts.
The peasants are knitting socks.
The peasants yawn.
The dung beetle was rolling its dung.
Would you light me a cigarette.
The dung beetle was rolling its dung.
You can go to hell as far as I.
The dung beetle was rolling its dung.
Later you won't remember if you don't.
The dung beetle was rolling its dung.
But otherwise you'll just have.
The dung beetle was rolling its dung.
But only unless you don't now.
The dung beetle was rolling its dung.
Well then possibly after all.
The dung beetle was rolling its dung.
Just like that and not or never.
The dung beetle was rolling its dung.
Is that so or isn't it.
The dung beetle was rolling its dung.
The turtledoves put it all behind them.

THE FOLDING CHAIRS

Our picnic gear consisted of a handsome folding table, a comfortable folding chair with armrests, a folding chair without armrests, two functioning and one nonfunctioning folding stools.

Messalina and Hanno occupied, by turns, the comfortable folding chair with armrests and the folding chair without armrests, while Hans, Petra and I occupied, by turns, the two functioning and one nonfunctioning folding stools. When Messalina was occupying the folding chair with armrests, I sat on the nonfunctioning folding stool, Hans and Petra sat on the functioning ones, and Hanno occupied the folding chair without armrests. When Hanno was occupying the folding chair with armrests, Hans sat on the nonfunctioning folding stool, Petra and I sat on the functioning ones, and Messalina occupied the folding chair without armrests. Petra was to take a turn on the nonfunctioning folding stool if she happened to lose a sock, or if she happened to have spilled the wine, or if she persisted in refusing to eat her pâté. But the one time she lost her sock, we didn't have the picnic things with us, and the one time she spilled the wine, Hans and I had just knocked over the table with all the plates and glasses, and when she refused to eat her pâté, Hanno said: if you won't eat your pâté, you'll have to sit on the broken chair next time. Thus the sequence of chair occupancy was disrupted and remained so throughout the remainder of our picnics, and the constellation that would have required the reciprocal exchange of folding chairs with and without armrests between Hanno and Messalina in conjunction with the similar exchange of the two functioning and one nonfunctioning folding stools among Hans, Petra and myself remained a plan to be put into action should Petra happen to lose a sock while a picnic was in progress, should she happen to spill the wine when Hans and I hadn't just knocked over the table with all the plates and glasses, and should she refuse to eat her pâté at a juncture when the possibility of applying the threatened punishment had not yet expired, that is, should she reject her portion of pâté during the penultimate picnic of the season.

These circumstances presented themselves already during the antepenultimate picnic. But now we didn't know which combination to adopt, whether Messalina should take the folding chair with armrests and Hanno the folding chair without armrests, with Hans and me taking seats upon the two functioning folding stools, leaving Petra the nonfunctioning one, or whether Hanno should take the folding chair with armrests and Messalina the folding chair without armrests.

I said: if from the beginning we had seen to it that Petra sat on the nonfunctioning folding stool whenever Messalina was sitting on the folding chair with armrests, Hanno on the folding chair without armrests, and Hans and I on the functioning folding stools, that I sat on the nonfunctioning folding stool whenever Messalina was sitting on the folding chair with armrests, Hanno on the folding chair without armrests, and Petra and Hans on the functioning folding stools, that Hans sat on the nonfunctioning folding stool whenever Messalina was sitting on the folding chair with armrests, Hanno on the folding chair without armrests, and Petra and I on the functioning folding stools, that Petra sat on the nonfunctioning folding stool whenever Hanno was sitting on the folding chair with armrests, Messalina on the folding chair without armrests, and Hans and I on the functioning folding stools, that I sat on the nonfunctioning folding stool

53

whenever Hanno was sitting on the folding chair with armrests, Messalina on the folding chair without armrests, and Hans and Petra on the functioning folding stools, that Hans sat on the nonfunctioning folding stool whenever Hanno was sitting on the folding chair with armrests, Messalina on the folding chair without armrests, and Petra and I on the functioning folding stools, and if we had consistently observed this sequence, then we wouldn't be in such a mess now.

Petra said: Uncle Luckeluckel is a conscientus and intellent person.

Lunch today featured pâté en croute à la campagne, jambon de Lorraine with olives, choucroute garnie out of a can, an especially potent camembert and two bottles of fourteen-percent Bordeaux rouge.

Petra didn't have to eat her pâté.

PLACE SIMIOT

Pito emerged from the rue des Enfants-assistés, ran across the
street from right to left and found himself on the place Simiot in
front of Julien's bar. He paused for a moment at Julien's corner,
raised his tail and then crossed the square diagonally from
corner to corner. In front of the boucherie, he lowered his tail
again, ran back across the street from left to right and vanished
in the direction of the rue Sainte Geneviève. The square
represented by the place Simiot was bisected diagonally by the
path of Pito's journey; it follows that the two catheti of the one
resulting triangle were marked out by the little grocery, the dairy
and the butcher shop, and the two catheti of the other by the
pharmacy, the pissoir and the neoclassical townhouses.

Monsieur Desgranges, notaire, closed his shutters because the
sun had appeared above the plane trees, with the result that the
papers pertaining to the firm of Fiche & Fabre, Spirits, now lay in
shadow. Monsieur Desgranges' great-grandfather had bought
glass beads and traveled with them to Senegal where he had
exchanged them for Senegalese. He had then transported the
Senegalese to Port-au-Prince, put them up for sale at the market-
place and used the proceeds to purchase a shipload of rum.
Having returned to Bordeaux with the rum, he bottled it for sale

and swapped the empty gallon jugs for glass beads. Today Monsieur Desgranges' house is ornamented by two columns with bases, fluted shafts and capitals; the entablature consists of architrave, frieze and cornice, all of it genuine, all of it stuccowork of the finest quality, the most elegant plaster.

On the far side of the hypotenuse, three men were moving beneath the plane trees; they were leaping about on the gravel; they were playing boules. The one with the corduroy trousers and blue undershirt squinted at the cochonnet, swung his right hand far behind him and delivered the first of his two balls. The one with cauliflower ears picked up his first boule from the ground, swiveled his wrist and lobbed the ball at the cochonnet. The three men walked over to the cochonnet; they bent over the constellation, and the one with false teeth said: je crois pas. Then they returned to their previous positions; the third aimed and threw. His boule struck the boule of the one with corduroy trousers, the balls clacked together and rolled away from the cochonnet. The men then delivered their second balls.

Pito returned from the rue Sainte Geneviève; he ran across the street from right to left and found himself on the place Simiot in front of the boucherie. He paused for a moment at the boucherie's corner, raised his tail and then crossed the square diagonally from corner to corner. At the exact center of square he stopped once more, for the door to Monsieur Desgranges' house had just clicked shut and Monsieur Desgranges appeared between the columns with a straw hat and an attaché case. He was fitted out in a light-gray suit, tan suede shoes and a thick attaché case thanks to his great-grandfather, who had exchanged glass beads for Senegalese and then brought back a shipload of rum from Guadeloupe in their stead. Monsieur Desgranges paused for a moment; he glanced at the cat who was now standing beside the streetlight and at the powdered sulfur strewn around the base of his columns. The one with corduroy trousers pulled back his arm for a swing, but the one with cauliflower ears grabbed his arm, and the third one said: watch out for the cat!

In front of the grocery, a chair had been set on the pavement, and upon it sat a woman holding a child on her lap. A second woman came out of the shop; she paused for a moment beside the chair, speaking to the child. The woman in the chair pointed at the cat; the child raised its arm up high and kicked its legs in the air. The woman standing beside the chair held a bag in her hand; she made some noises and with her free hand patted the child's cheeks. From behind the pissoir, three children emerged, a boy and two girls. The boy was carrying a box under his arm; he ran past the pharmacy and Julien's, making for the door of Au Myosotis; the girls ran after him. In front of the shop, the boy knelt down in the gutter, placed the box on the ground and opened it. The girls bent over the box. They shrieked and leapt back a few steps. Something sprang out of the box, scurried along the gutter and disappeared into the canal. Cattycorner from Chez Julien, the clinking of beads could be heard; two men stepped onto the sidewalk and shook hands. Then they turned their backs on one another; one of them walked off in the direction of Au Myosotis, the other in the direction of the pharmacy. The façades of the pharmacy, the neoclassical townhouses and Julien's now lay in the sun. The triglyph friezes gleamed in the light, the squashed cushions of the capitals cast their shadows, the entablatures above the windows displayed their garlands of laurels.

The man with false teeth reached for the cochonnet, picked it up and tossed it in a different direction. Monsieur Desgranges exited his portal of Doric columns, turned to the right and, at the corner of the building where the catheti of the neighborhood triangle intersected, described a right angle to the left. When he appeared again behind the pissoir, Pito had also begun to move again, so that the two of them, had they both wished to enter the rue des Enfants-assistés, would have met somewhere between Julien's corner and Au Myosotis. The cat fell into a slow trot, but Monsieur Desgranges was unable to increase his speed without cause, since the child on the woman's lap was still thrashing about.

On the far side of the hypotenuse, the three men were leaping about again; they had begun a new game; the balls grated against the gravel. The cochonnet now lay halfway between the streetlamp and the corner with the dairy; the men had turned their backs to the pissoir and Monsieur Desgranges and held their heads bent over the difficult combinations. The one with the corduroy trousers and the blue undershirt was moving his index finger back and forth; then he squatted down and with his outstretched hand measured the distance of two balls from the cochonnet. The one with cauliflower ears took a step forward; he studied the distance of the two balls from the cochonnet and then described a 90° arc so as to gain a new perspective from this position. The one with false teeth shook his head; he pointed to the cochonnet and said: je crois pas. The men, their second balls in hand, walked back to the throw line and then delivered their balls.

At this moment, Monsieur Desgranges had reached the beginning of the rue des Enfants-assistés. With his straw hat and his attaché case, he strode beneath banded architraves and cornice-topped consoles that would not have existed if his great-grandfather had not brought a shipload of rum from the Antilles and sold it. Monsieur Desgranges strode valiantly forward; the three children with the box crossed his path; the child on the woman's lap was still flailing about.

Pito had stopped at Au Myosotis; he sat at the edge of the gutter to allow Monsieur Desgranges to enter the rue des Enfants-assistés ahead of him. Then he raised his tail, observed Monsieur Desgranges from the rear and crossed over to Julien's bar. At Julien's corner he lowered his tail again, ran across the street from right to left, and exited the place Simiot.

THE TORSO

The sunhat was hanging upon a neoclassical torso. Have a look at that, Hans said.

We had a look. But does a thing look the way it looks when one is looking at it, or rather does a thing one is looking at not look the way it looks when one is looking at it? Most of the time it doesn't look the way it looks, though there are cases in which a thing really does look the way it looks.

Most things don't look the way they look. But there are things that do look the way they look. There aren't any things that don't look the way they don't look, but there are things that don't look the way they look.

This one looked the way it looked. We would have been glad to see it not looking the way it looked, but it looked the way it looked. It's true there aren't many things that look the way they look, but most things don't look the way they look. And since we had set our hearts on this thing not looking the way it looked, it looked the way it looked.

The sunhat was hanging on a neoclassical torso. And since we had looked at it in this way and not some other way, we couldn't see the point of its looking the way it looked, but this thing undeniably looked the way it looked, and we ought to have been able to see the point, since it looked the way it looked, of its looking not the way it didn't look but rather the way it did.

There was, as has already been said, a sunhat hanging on a neoclassical torso. Admittedly it was an overripe day with an air like stifling bedclothes and a full-breasted sun as we set off on our drive to the Sauterne. First we worked our way up along the Garonne, winding through the vineyard-covered hillsides of Graves and gradually ascending the plateau of Bazadais. Finally the château Yquem appeared on a hilltop above us, burnt brown in the glare. All around us, in the light filtering down into the vine-yards, the vines were sighing, the grapes were still hard and full, but the vintners walked shaking their heads among the rows of vines.

Our point of view appeared to have lost all perspective, so we focused on seeing things, from where we stood, not in some way they didn't look but rather the way they did.

We were intending to visit the sculptor Jacob at château Pajot, we found the house at last, it lay there broiling in the midday sun, but Jacob was out. Madame Baron met us at the gate. A Persian named Twist was prancing about at her feet; and there was this sunhat hanging on a neoclassical torso.

It isn't easy to see the point of hanging a sunhat on a neoclassical torso. Even with it looking the way it looked, we didn't see the point of its looking the way it looked. Not that we were unwilling to see that it isn't proper to hang a sunhat on a neoclassical torso, or that the torso had seen better days, days in which it had looked the way it looked as a neoclassical torso sans sunhat, which is what had made it look like a neoclassical torso in the first place, the absence of the hat; or that the sunhat was made of woven straw and not the same material as the torso, for we are inclined to forgive not only a sunhat for being a sunhat, because we have a weakness for sunhats, we'd have forgiven a Panama hat or a top hat the same thing; no, what we couldn't see the point of was the neoclassical torso.

And here in turn it was not the fact that we didn't see the point of its being a neoclassical torso in its capacity as an object of our age, although it is difficult to see how it could be neoclassical as an object of our age, which doesn't mean a person who makes a neoclassical torso in our age cannot get away with making a neoclassical torso if it pleases him to make a neoclassical torso. No, the thing we couldn't see the point of is that it was a neoclassical torso, that is, that it was a torso that was neoclassical.

The longlegged granddaughter led us into the salon. Madame Baron brought us wine and crackers.

The sunhat was hanging on the trunk, but this trunk was no leftover from antiquity that had lost head and limbs in the course of time but nonetheless continued to subsist as a whole, and it didn't appear to be what remained of some destroyed work of art, as sculptors say of genuine classical torsi; nor was it one of those figures, fragmentary by design, that are created by modern sculptors who know that a man without head or face is not a man but who nonetheless create men lacking heads and limbs because what they want to create is not men per se but rather merely the plastic form, for which head and arms are superfluous; it was a torso that was neoclassical, that is to say, it was a trunk without a head and without arms and without legs, but it wasn't alive, as is said of the debris of antiquity and the by design headless figures of modern artists, but rather neoclassical.

Madame Baron filled our glasses and wished us good health. The front edge of the sunhat was resting against the nipples of the neoclassical torso. If the torso hadn't been neoclassical, one might have said a naked woman had fallen asleep and her hat had slipped from her head onto her chest.

Or might it have been something that only looked as if it looked the way it looked?

THE ECCENTRIC

C'est quelque original, her father repeated to her several times, as Madame de S-y is reported to have said when she caught a glimpse from her balcony one afternoon of a stranger cutting across the fields.

He's an eccentric, said her father, as Madame de S-y is reported to have said, after she'd encountered him while out for a stroll and, as is reported, went on to confess that any other figure she might thus have encountered would have given her the most dreadful fright and made her run for home, if it hadn't been for a certain noble expression of pain imprinted on his features that had won her over.

An eccentric, she is said to have reported her father saying, a prisoner of war, more or less a fugitive, for there he was wandering aimlessly though gardens and fields, on his lips a form of French that neither she nor her father could have recognized as correct. In a transport of joy, as her father later told her, as Madame de S-y is reported to have said, he had hastened with buoyant steps toward a company of twenty-four major and minor divinities, for the most part copies of ancient statuary, a Neptune by Giovanni da Bologna at their center, arranged upon a balustrade bordering a pool constructed in lieu of a lawn at the center of the park which he, the one to whom Madame de S-y is said to have recounted these events, had not himself had the good fortune to see, and he circled this pool, wandering from one statue to the next, so as to remain standing the longest before the most beautiful one.

He's eccentric, leave him in peace, her father shouted to the garde champêtre, whose wish it would have been to eject him from the garden, as Madame de S-y is said to have described this occurrence, so the chronicler's report.

Behold this Aglaia, see how she smiles upon me and makes me her prisoner; it is not only her owner for whom she smiles, said the stranger, so the report.

It is a Pomona, said her father, so the report.

No, an Aglaia, the stranger insisted; the water here ought to be clearer, like the waters of the Cephissus or the flood of the Erechtheus upon the Acropolis, for it is unworthy of the clear gods to see themselves mirrored in so dark a glass.

But, her father objected, so the report.

Alas, sighed the stranger, so the report, we are not in Greece.

Are you a Greek? her father asked.

On the contrary, the stranger said, I am a German.

On the contrary? her father repeated, so the report, is a German the opposite of a Greek?

Yes, the German answered, all of us are.

He is a German, her father said, an eccentric, as Madame de S-y is said to have reported, one whose words had made a strong impression upon her father, for henceforth whenever he ordered the pool to be cleaned, he made a habit of adding in jest: so that the water will be as clear as the waters of the Cephissus or the flood of the Erechtheus upon the Acropolis.

All of them developed a great fondness for the eccentric, Madame de S-y is said to have reported to the chronicler, and so they were pleased, after the stranger had accepted without formalities her father's invitation to enter the house, to see him march up to a sofa and lie down there to take his rest. After a refreshing slumber, he joined them at table and partook of the wine with increasing good cheer, as her father later related to her, as Madame de S-y is reported to have said, so the chronicler tells us. With dreaming eyes he gazed through the window facing the garden containing the stone divinities arranged upon the balustrade bordering the pool constructed in lieu of a lawn in the middle of the park which he, the one to whom Madame de S-y is said to have recounted these occurrences, had not himself had the good fortune to see, pondering a distance which none of them, as Madame de S-y is reported to have said, as her father related to her, so the chronicler informs us, were able to see.

The beautiful Garonne and the gardens of Bordeaux there, the stranger said, so the report, on grape-clad hills, where down comes the Dordogne.

He's mad, her aunt whispered, so the report.

He's a German, said her father, so the report, I like him, he's eccentric.

Together with the splendid Garonne as wide as the sea the river moves out, the stranger said, so the report, got up from the table and reached out both arms to the window.

THE STONES OF M. DE MONTAIGNE

(Lately I retired to my house resolved that, in so far as I could, I would cease to concern myself with anything except the passing in rest and retirement of the little time I still have to live.)

I was seated beneath an elm tree near the terrace, my back propped against its trunk, and held the book on my knees. The others were lying upon the lap robe spread out beneath the plane trees beside the sandstone bench. Hans was sketching, and Petra was gathering pebbles. There was a strong scent of fennel and thyme, though I was unable to determine which was the fennel smell and which the thyme. I turned the page and continued reading.

(The water that M. de Montaigne drank on Tuesday induced three bowel movements and was discharged from his system by midday. He noted no other effects from it, except that his urine smelled of sweet violet.) Hanno said: can you smell the thyme? Hans was sketching, Petra was gathering pebbles, Messalina smelled the thyme. I had once more reached the lower right-hand edge of the page, turned it, and resumed reading at the upper left.

M. de Montaigne stood upon the terrace of the castle. He wore a sunhat and a cravat with a Windsor knot. He strode across the sandstone blocks of the terrace, his hands crossed upon his buttocks. With his pointed shoes he struck a stone of moderate size which went skidding across the slabs of sandstone, struck the raised edge of the terrace wall, rebounded and rolled back in front of M. de Montaigne's feet.

(In the course of the day, M. de Montaigne passed two stones and a great many granules. He clearly perceived the activity of each stone and followed its passage through his urinary tract and nether parts. He did, however, pass two smaller stones located in the bladder, later voiding sand several times, while maintaing the conviction that he still had the stone in his bladder along with others which he believed he had felt descending.)

M. de Montaigne bent to retrieve the stone that had rolled in front of his feet. As he bent over, his sunhat slid into his face. Squatting there, he lost himself in the contemplation of the stone.

(Upon rising, he passed a stone of moderate size which broke easily into pieces.)

M. de Montaigne picked up the stone and studied it attentively. (On the outside it was yellowish, but more of a whitish color inside.)

M. de Montaigne allowed the stone to slip from right hand to left. He touched it on all sides with the fingertips of his right hand. Then he walked to the edge of the terrace and leaned against the balustrade.

Far below in the valley, the Dordogne was making a curve and flowing towards Sainte-Foy. It was early in the afternoon. That's why I was sitting beneath the elm and the others were lying beneath the plane trees. (Now the heat was beginning to make itself felt and the chirping of crickets could be heard.)

The water level of the Dordogne was low, but M. de Montaigne followed the river's course carefully with his eyes. (The water was having an effect, before as well as behind, and he voided an insignificant quantity of grains.)

I was sitting beneath the elm, but the others lay beneath the plane trees beside the sandstone bench. This meant that the M.

de Montaigne who stood at the balustrade of the castle terrace following with his eyes the course of the river whose water was flowing only thinly in a curve towards Sainte-Foy was not the M. de Montaigne who had discharged all his water and was smelling of sweet violet. This meant also, as a consequence, that the M. de Montaigne who had kicked a stone against the terrace wall with his pointed shoe was not the M. de Montaigne who had passed a stone upon rising. Therefore the stone of moderate size that M. de Montaigne was investigating with his fingertips was not the stone of moderate size of M. de Montaigne that, once the latter had gotten up and passed it, broke easily into pieces. And if the M. de Montaigne who as M. de Montaigne, standing with his sunhat and Windsor knot above the valley of the Dordogne with a stone in his hand, was not identical to the M. de Montaigne for whom, as M. de Montaigne, the water had had its effect both before and behind, and he no longer had a stone, this should by no means suggest it is a question of two different MM. de Montaigne.

For the father of the M. de Montaigne who upon rising had passed the abovementioned stone of moderate size that broke easily into pieces was himself a bearer of stones which, like his son, M. de Montaigne, he voided at regular intervals, so that the M. de Montaigne who stood at the terrace balustrade holding a stone of moderate size in his hand might perfectly well also have been be a bearer and voider of stones like the M. de Montaigne whose water had smelled of sweet violet. And this in turn permits the conclusion that the M. de Montaigne who had passed the stones might also have conveyed stones towards the balustrade of his castle terrace with a pointed shoe, just like the M. de Montaigne with the sunhat and the Windsor knot, who was surely a bearer not merely of the stone he now held in his hand as he observed the Dordogne valley.

There were no stones of the MM. de Montaigne if they were not those of my M. de Montaigne and those of the M. de Montaigne of the others; and even in this case it was not unambiguous what sort of stones were meant, since on the one hand stones are stones, while on the other, stones are by no means stones if one considers that these stones might well have the same composition and form, but that one can not only bear but also void these stones of the same composition and form in quite different ways.

M. de Montaigne raised the hand in which he was holding the stone high above his head and hurled it over the balustrade of the terrace into the valley of the Dordogne. (There followed a thick, hard, long stone in one piece whose passage through the organ took between five and six hours.)

If the two MM. de Montaigne were alike, then they were not identical to one another, since the two MM. de Montaigne passed stones in two different ways, in other words, the two stones were passed by the MM. de Montaigne in two different ways.

If the two stones were alike, then they were not identical to one another, since the two stones were passed by the two MM. de Montaigne in two different ways, in other words, the two MM. de Montaigne passed stones in two different ways.

Across the gravel, the castle's tour guide now approached the others beneath the plane trees and said: M. de Montaigne's study is now at your disposal. I shut my book beneath the elm and went to rejoin the others.

M. de Montaigne turned his back on the terrace balustrade and strode across the slabs of sandstone back to the house. The tour guide said: M. de Montaigne is just going into his study. He can now work undisturbed.

We followed the tour guide into the study of M. de Montaigne, which was now at our disposal, while M. de Montaigne was able to proceed to his study in order to pass the time there free from all disturbances.

THE BEACH

When the summer's crop of bunnies is ready for slaughter and is shipped off by the busload to the beaches of the Atlantic coastline, concupiscent consumers appear in droves beneath the palm trees and pines of the Second Empire hotels.

We loaded the car with the beach gear: swim trunks to cover up willies and balls, bathing suits for mounts of Venus and breasts, Nivea for skins, brushes for hair, folding chairs for buttocks, sunshades for gray matter. We drove to the Arcachon basin. Every tree along the road was an ace of spades, and we raced through the entire flush in an hour. *Pessac, ch.-l. de c. (Gironde), arr. de Bordeaux; 19 200 h. (15 000 aggl.). Vins; aciérie. Gujan-Mestras, comm. de la Gironde, arr. de Bordeaux; 5000 h. (3800 aggl.) Ostréiculture. Teste (La), anc. La Texte-de-Buch, ch.-l. de c. (Gironde), arr. de Bordeaux, sur le bassin d'Arcachon; 11 300 h. (6900 aggl.) (Testerins).* Children's homes, old folks' homes, convalescent homes, reformatories, vacation homes. No piping shepherds of Provence (Calendal! Calendal!), no strutting flamingos of Camargue (mirrored as in Fragonard), no prancing fauns of Esterel (hard by the aqueducts up hairpin turns behind the Tanneron), no powdery butterflies from Sérignan (in the Hermas daily except Mondays), no stone torsi from Orange (before this most beautiful wall in his kingdom), no dreaming Phaeacians of the Levant (may sweet slumber o'ertake me).

69

We arrived around noon, drove over to Françoise's and dug into her crabs. Françoise had a smallish something lying in the cradle and appeared to be in fine fettle all 'round. Her breasts were like pears, but it was her crabs we dug into.

The bathing niche of Arcachon was drowsing beneath the mild sou'-wester. Oyster nets stagnated just off the coast. A few sails were bobbing in the wind. In front of us, a fishing boat tugged at its anchor. We dived down under the boat, but the soup was too salty. Right off we smelled a rat, something was rotten. This water was not to our liking. It had a brownish cast to it, and the foam floating on its surface appeared to derive from local products of digestion. The fishermen sat in formation. They had no bait on their hooks. Nonetheless, they pulled fish after fish out of the water.

We let ourselves dry in the sun, then packed up our gear, swim trunks for willies and balls, bathing suits for mounts of Venus and breasts, Nivea for skins, brushes for hair, folding chairs for buttocks, sunshades for gray matter, and strolled around the corner to where the open sea began.

There the meat was spread out on the mats to grill. The girls had their legs stretched out in front of them. The men kept their thighs together. An old woman was knitting socks. Children were playing with a schnauzer. He was sniffing at a plastic bag. The children emptied a bucket of water over the schnauzer's back. The schnauzer shook himself, spraying the water over the sand. The water turned the sand dark for a moment, then it was white again. At regular intervals the surf struck the shore. Wherever the breakers hit the sand, it turned dark yellow for a moment. An old man in long trousers was walking along the beach. His trouser hems trailed in the sand. The schnauzer forgot the plastic bag and began chasing the old man. Its ears flew back, flinging drops of water into the air.

No piping shepherds of Provence, no strutting flamingos of Camargue, no prancing fauns of Esterel, no powdery butterflies from Sérignan, no stone torsi from Orange, no dreaming Phaeacians of the Levant.

Suddenly a whistle split the air. A man was walking through the sand. He wore blue shorts, a white shirt and a blue-and-white sailor's cap. The whistle hung on a cord against his white shirt. Upon the shirt stood the word: police. The man was carrying a snorkel and fins in his left hand. With his right, he shooed the kids out of the water, pointed at the red flag flying above the weather station and inserted the whistle between his lips. He had eyes only for the water and the red flag. He swung his snorkel and fins back and forth and vanished among the flesh-covered mats.

Behind the beach grass lay Arcachon with its Second Empire hotels, *ch.-l. de c. (Gironde), arr. de Bordeaux, sur le bassin d'Arcachon, formé par le golfe de Gascogne; 14 900 h. (Arcachonnais). Station balnéaire et hivernale. Ostréiculture.* Here the butchers with their accoutrements celebrate the rite of slaughter when the summer's crop of bunnies is shipped off by the busload to the beaches of the Atlantic coastline. The display cases contained an admirable array of goods: smoked ham and grilled loins, delicate breast cuts, ribs with bacon, and all of this garnished with Russian egg salad and Italian greens, not to mention the German pig's trotters and fried meat patties. No piping shepherds of Provence, no strutting flamingos of Camargue, no prancing fauns of Esterel, no powdery butterflies from Sérignan, no stone torsi from Orange, no dreaming Phaeacians of the Levant. Swim trunks for panpipes, bathing suits for flamingo strides, Nivea for fauns' tails, brushes for butterfly powder, folding chairs for torso stones, sunshades for Phaeacian dreams.

Costly liturgical investments for a gastronomical mass. We brought our bunnies with us and devoured them in the shade.

71

THE ODALISQUE

In the sand behind the dune we set up camp. Hanno and Messalina lay down beneath the sunshade on the colorfast beach towel. Hans and I applied lotion to each other's backs. Petra, who was hopping around in the beach grass in her bikini, said: Papa, there's a lady over there who's all black.

She was lying on her belly just a few steps away. Her skin was terra di siena from her nape to her heels. The narrow cloth band of the bra running across her back and the triangle of her panties which covered the point where her two buttocks converged in the dark central furrow may perhaps have concealed a few square centimeters of white skin.

Hans took a drag on his cigarette. I polished the lenses of my sunglasses with my handkerchief.

The brown-skinned woman turned over and now lay on her back. She had shaved away the hair beneath her arms. The somewhat larger front triangle of her panties and the two bits of cloth that comprised her bra now concealed only those body parts specified in §183 I of the German criminal code as inappropriate for public display.

Hans inhaled desperately, but his fire had gone out. I interrupted the cleaning of my sunglasses, retrieved the matches from my pants pocket and relit his cigarette.

The brown-skinned woman had her eyes closed and was breathing softly, peacefully. Her flesh was firm beneath her skin, and with every breath her bra rose and fell. Her thighs were pressed tightly together, but her hands lay some distance from her panties in the sand. At the center of her belly was a black crater. Her umbilical cord had been properly tied off — the papilla where the cord had been attached could not be seen. She was just lying there, we didn't know why. She was already maximally tan. The sea was boiling. Atop the weather station, the green flag had been raised. For her there was no swimming to be done, no chatting, no more tanning. She just lay there. (The object of our investigations is always man, who is undeniably a physical being.)

Hans was going full steam ahead. He inflated his nostrils and blew out the air audibly. He took a comb from the plastic bag and put a part in his hair. I stood up. Messalina said: what's the matter? I said: my right foot fell asleep. I positioned myself with my legs far apart. (I have a strong and thick-set body, my face is full but not fat. My legs and chest are covered copiously with hair.)

Messalina said: there's no point taking pictures, the camera has to be facing the sun. I sat back down.

The brown-skinned woman was still lying on her back without moving. She wasn't dead, she was alive. She wasn't only alive, but also just this moment perhaps not exactly but it might if one had taken a different and still assuming a proper and this ticklish avoided with many various one might even if instead but one must and doesn't know if there's anything behind it.

What's wrong with you, said Messalina. I said: I don't know what's going on with my foot.

The odalisque stretched her limbs and rolled back over on her stomach. Just this moment perhaps not. Fine. Nothing to object to in that. Not exactly, shall we say. But it might. That much is certain. It might if one had taken a different. That much let's agree on. And still had. No mice biting the thread there. Assuming a proper. (A thorny proposition.) And this ticklish. We're not going to stick our necks out on this account. Not that. Perfectly clear. Avoided with many. Very well then. With many various. Also good. That lies in the nature of the thing. One might even. Through thick and thin. Even if instead. But to let it get under your skin instead? Let's not forget that. Don't you think? Fine. One must. But want to bet that? Don't know. This much is perhaps beyond doubt. Don't know if. It's worth considering that. Don't know if there's anything behind it. This is definitely worth considering.

What's the matter with your foot, Messalina said. I don't know, I said, it prickles. (One goes to work on his eyes, the second on his ears, the third on his mouth; no part of him is spared abuse.)

The brown odalisque lay on her belly. Now it was her shoulder blades rising and falling. Her skin was perfectly smooth and gleaming. Between her buttocks and her thighs lay a tiny fold. She lay there, nothing in particular on her mind. She wasn't swimming, she wasn't chatting, she wasn't even tanning any longer. She just lay there.

SUNBATHING

Locate lounge-chair facilitate repose insinuate falsehoods
substantiate impressions communicate message tolerate
admonitions obviate questions state name susurrate sounds
enunciate syllables articulate words modulate voice mitigate
doubts accelerate response explicate solution demonstrate example
repudiate intentions adumbrate inclinations confabulate signs
dilate eye advocate scenario simulate soul formulate wishes
prognosticate bliss animate limbs titillate fingers stimulate nose
assimilate scents consecrate strength placate irritations motivate
caresses invalidate objections confiscate hands accentuate
resolve circumnavigate navel pollinate eyelash interrogate
shoulder palpitate muscle cultivate toe meditate hip masticate
lips infiltrate thigh resuscitate nipple permeate loins celebrate
breasts penetrate armpit investigate teeth perforate nape elevate
calves dominate back violate hair emancipate legs exhilarate
tongue aggravate offense annihilate defense illustrate plans
concentrate means create traps facilitate position compensate
location denigrate ascent accommodate descent obfuscate
judgment imprecate envious inundate body precipitate suddenly
fulminate fierily inebriate shyly prestidigitate slyly reciprocate
firmly escalate wildly saturate lasciviously captivate wordlessly
procrastinate tenderly perpetuate sensually exacerbate
relentlessly participate willingly deviate resourcefully speculate
senselessly replicate rapturously collaborate handily elate

spiritedly ululate furiously satiate straightforwardly remonstrate sourly negate sensibly implicate trickily congratulate sneakily deflate heatedly sedate tempestuously jubilate victoriously commemorate guilelessly mediate gently vacate gingerly

THE DUNE

The dune had already taken a step into the pine woods. It now was standing with one foot just before the terrace of the seaside resort.

Just one more quick beer, Hanno said.

She waded through the sand, from which there were only a few blades of grass sticking out, and clomped across the wooden planks of the terrace. She turned around and said: it's so high.

Hans unbuckled his sandals, took Petra by the hand and gazed up at the dune's summit.

Messalina said: are you coming or not?

I said: you can't see the top.

Hans took a step forward but then sank into the sand up to his ankles and slid half a step back.

We'll have to take that into account, he said, and we calculated that for every two steps we took, one would be in vain.

What a waste, Messalina said.

After we had wasted ninety-six steps, we collapsed to our knees. The angular crystals were scraping against our ankles. Our feet hurt. Our legs kept making cracking sounds. Our skin was on fire. Sharp pains went shooting through our loins. It was all we could do to extricate ourselves.

O merciful heavens, Hans said.

Tut, tut, said Messalina.

Messalina stared holes in the heavens, she let her eyes drift across them, winked at them, smiled at them, took the heavens in her arms, called them friendly names, gave them a warning, scolded them.

When we had wasted one hundred ninety-two steps, we gazed over the crest of the dune. Before us, the sea lay spread out along a South Seas coastline. Sand as far as the eye could see. Pine trees trailing off into the distance. Water asserting its presence. Behind us, the woods swallowed up everything.

No village lay spread out before us. No road trailing off into the distance. No farm asserting its presence.

It was no longer the heavens Messalina was staring holes in, letting her eyes drift across, winking at, smiling at, taking in her arms, calling friendly names, warning and scolding, but rather the sea.

The sea had lost its composure. It had taken leave of its senses and was thrashing about blindly. It bellowed and raged. It poked its head up over the woods, kicked at the dune, bit into the sand.

Petra threatened the sea, kicked at it, ran away from it, threw a stone at the sea, stuck out her tongue at it, joked around with the sea, cuddled it, squatted down in it.

The sea bared its teeth and spat. In no time it had foam on its lips. It was boiling and leaping out of its skin. The waves rolled against the shore and weltered in the sand.

It was no longer the sea Petra was threatening, kicking at, running away from, throwing a stone at, sticking out her tongue at, joking around with, cuddling and squatting down in, but rather the sand.

She took off her shoes and socks.

Papa, she said, look, I don't have legs any more.

Papa let his face dissolve.

Well, he said, don't I have an adorable child?

He began wrestling with the kid, rolled around in the sand, drizzled sand over his own head, buried his arms in it, rammed his left leg into it, scooped it into his trouser pockets, caressed the sand, bit into the sand, flogged the sand.

But the kid's right sock was nowhere to be found.

It was no longer the sand Papa was rolling around in, drizzling over his own head, burying his arms in, ramming his left leg into, scooping into his trouser pockets, caressing, biting into and flogging, but rather the kid.

The sea was beside itself. The western wind leapt over the dune. The surf howled and roared. It slammed into the shore, flailing away at the sand.

Hans said: That's enough!

The kid quit wailing. She had located her sock. She said: Papa, now you can roll around in the sand some more.

But the sun was shaking its head and peering over the crest of the dune at the seaside resort. The dune had taken another step into the pine woods. It now stood with both feet before the terrace of the seaside resort.

Just one more quick beer, we saw Hanno saying as we waved from above with our shirts.

THE WATERCOLOR

On the dune at Pyla, Hans made an astonishing discovery. Around five o'clock, the water's coloration modulated. The sea changed its tune. A play of colors to mark the hour of seduction.

The blue stopped the yellow in its tracks. But all that emerged was this one narrow streak. Beyond the streak, a bit of green had coalesced. Perfect stasis and peace. The blue and yellow kept dipping into the green, fixing it in place. This self-satisfied, earthly calm. The bourgeois green wasn't making any headway. Indolently it spread and eventually swallowed up the streak of yellow. The sun shot a sudden ray into the dunes. But the blue immediately siphoned off the red. A cindery violet was fading into nothing, and Messalina began to laugh. The yellow washed out the ink blot, and Messalina said, now everything's green.

Hans unpacked his watercolors, opened the water bottle and moistened the paper. Then he poked around in the cakes of paint and drizzled blue and yellow onto the paper. Triangles and circles emerged. The green broth dispersed. You're colorblind, I said, there's no green there. But he dipped his brush into the paint and applied a thick swath of green. Kandinsky's string ensemble.

Slowly the round the warm the eccentric yellow approached in a triangle, and quickly the angular the cold the concentric blue retreated in a circle. Hans went to town with Indian yellow and indigo. He didn't let the image blow smoke in his eyes. Messalina was laughing again. The colors all flowed together. Slowly the round the warm the eccentric yellow approached in a circle, and quickly the angular the cold the concentric blue retreated in a triangle. He sprinkled the page with water, churned up the chrome oxide, got the cobalt flowing and scattered ochre in between. Quickly the round the warm the eccentric yellow retreated in a triangle, and slowly the angular the cold the concentric blue approached in a circle. Now he added ultramarine to the umber and watched it disperse in the water. Outside, an incursion of red. He paid no attention. Inside the picture, the hodgepodge was dissolving into green. Quickly the round the warm the eccentric yellow retreated in a circle, and slowly the angular the cold the concentric blue approached in a triangle. He dipped his brush in the water, emptied out the little tin of cadmium yellow, made circles in the Paolo Veronese, sprinkled and washed. Slowly the angular the cold the concentric blue approached in a triangle, and quickly the round the warm the eccentric yellow retreated in a circle. He dissolved the Prussian blue in the water and introduced a single drop of it into the picture. Slowly the angular the cold the concentric blue approached in a circle, and quickly the round the warm the eccentric yellow retreated in a triangle. The drop of Prussian blue sat above and to the right of the picture's center. It was garishly bright. Its edges were becoming saw-toothed in the water. The drop was the cogwheel driving the whole sluggish brew. Quickly the angular the cold the concentric blue retreated in a triangle and slowly the round the warm the eccentric yellow approached in a circle. The blue was now flowing in streams. It collided with the yellow and came to rest. There were still bits and flecks of it in its pure form everywhere, only gradually did it mix with the other colors. But quickly the angular the cold the concentric blue retreated in a circle and slowly the round the warm the eccentric yellow approached in a triangle, becoming angular and cold as he plunged into the chrome so as to mark out the line of the horizon. He had seen green. (Since he was he and I was I.) Middling-to-deep notes on the violin. Play of colors. Kandinsky's string ensemble.

Personally, it makes me see red.

THE DOUBTS OF M. DE MONTAIGNE

What is there to say about childbirth and kidneys?

One should always show respect for one's prick and goolies. For the reason that it requires frequent service. Verify the quality of the blade and the sheath. In the case of women, it is mainly the ability to fly. If the sheath is gone, you'll scarcely pay a farthing for the blade. Shirt, bed canopy, dagger. All these are accoutrements, not qualities. Measure one. Drain it off. Ours we ought rather the one he the one. His task to. To us he since all is correctly. Therefore I put great store in being presented with wild fruits. Such fruits described which. Of this, only a general, indistinct image. Wild in the sense one speaks of wild fruits. If one does not thus with women. Errors and failings are kept secret. Existing before it appears. What is now to be felt and to. Unseemly and harmful brought to each of us by wishes. If at least his paternal love. How ghastly that. Of his child as well and that she.

Why does the rumbling of the stomach function?

Everything within us is wind. It's just a question of. To which must be added that this wind is cleverer than we are. In his childhood, he presents the most surprising and various aspects. He is content with his calling. We are always somehow hovering above reality. He enjoys constancy and endurance. When struck with colic, he indulges himself beneath the curtain. There is in fact nothing else in it but wind. And a hundred who would cast a fog upon our judgment. Whether we perceive it as pleasant or unpleasant is in fact no different. The so-called fair sex surely not. For the most part not, but rather. Not equally in consequence of. Not the position without her. Not embroidered with gold and pearls. Little of the whole while at the same time. Nothing instead of whose for.

Why not?

A father does not speak willingly of the fantasies of a man. When the hump is clearly visible, one notes the outermost crust of knowledge. While the others are singing their own praises, they deceive and deform the necklace of things. This induces blindness. To have appear and none other but ourselves. Fantasy created man. His riches. His power. His stilts. A lovely castle. What he himself has to offer you can see from also out of or only in having something. But I find, when I consider the matter properly, things to be present that give off very little when one is in need of. The inhabitants of this far-flung land always in the future, so that they will not with this windbag who I, so to speak, not seeing the item. But fate and destiny do not encompass them. His son shall fright us.

Where must we attempt to relieve him of his strangeness?

Where the view is widespread that the soul is mortal. Where men carry their loads upon their heads. Where fleas are bitten to death. Where the women standing up and the men like a flea with their nails. Where women from neighboring tribes assuage bitterness with garden work. Where all one's life neither nor. Where those who if not to that of which as. I have not. They make an equally senseless. Shall we weep with so many more years yet will live, as weeping over that we long ago. Has preserved me. One does for an. One observing brings back around I as the one with whom it. He once defined his profession as. She and that in full consciousness life to which he precisely to this end.

Is life gay and replete with good health?

If we have not, one hundred years hence, were not. Without effort I can take my leave of anything except myself. Death is among the greatest indignities. In order to approach it nothing other than so often as. Human beings suffer from anxieties and hopes. The consequences of a conception are put to death. Then I am saddened not to have finished the garden. Without making a secret of it, I can see as well as any other that everything I do not write down in detail goes the usual road. Communicating to another what. But only of this do I. And not to him or those yet to come. But that I and few still are yet to have in these.

Why does one suffer ornament and splendor to go to pot?

Because man is a beast deserving pity. Whenever one makes the purchase of an animal, one has the seller display the beast's salient points. When I think of how human beings look naked, it seems to me that the invention of clothing was more necessary for us than for any other creature. The essence of things is kept wrapped up and concealed when it comes down to judging its worth. For a greyhound, speed. For a falcon, imagination. With an emperor, we appraise the hair. With a king, the nails. Princes do not sleep any differently. A manor lord gets scotched. A rich man slices counterfeit fruit. A high official shouts out of the flames. A private individual has death on his mind. A rhetorician from antiquity has no objections. Tyrants powder their crowns the way monkeys do. A peasant is happy when he can rustle and sough. A martyr has a stone malady in his soul. A poor man finds small things large upon his shoulders. A serf is after all a man. The artisans of beauty transform head scabs into sweetmeats in the French style. Who deck out the women. And appear. And one considers it carefully. And call.

And lay aside. And place. And what one thinks of. And a. Show where the girls can give themselves and be eliminated that to need where one sees how.

What can one see behind virgins?

Without income one cannot. Burns their sexual parts open. She is even. Sufficiently broiled on this side. Sometimes, however, reaching to the bones. Then jab your finger right in there. Cause less harm than the usual word-twisters. Not widespread. It lies in the nature of pain as one sees. But as deep as I possibly can. Every thing has a hundred faces. If it is long, a straight oar appears curved in the water. If it is short, it isn't deep. When he is heated in his manner, his appetite impresses. The moment he becomes unbearable, let the other side have its turn. If he hangs, you won't have to put up with him much longer. In a crouching position in the water he will succumb. When he shows himself publicly, just stroke it lightly from time to time. If a hundred limbs are fluttering, hack them off. Or just take one at a time. There's really no difference in the end. But shelter them from sunburn and rain. Dreadful women physically my him us at him to accustom him us in our sketched out again and again. The one that she considers us so sad, that girls are purchased from nature to whom they often already in the other. They deprive us of the opportunity. Perhaps then only from that point no longer. As much credit as marriage from the wise men who bring marriage. Each individual thing of beauty only through their. Not, to be sure, therefore as it to me also. As I am, you not being to the things themselves. Couples distinguish between a person and a person. According to qualities that are precisely not according. Not only our eyes but the way they when. These every time that upon his that are as we he they us.

THE GRAPES

When I think back on these two weeks — we hadn't done it (in order to know how many steps around the Santa Rotunda measures, or how luxurious the intimate apparel of Signora Livia is, or by how much the length or breadth of a Nero's head in some ancient ruin exceeds that of the one imprinted on some other coin) — then I see the five of us walking through the iron gate into the courtyard, where Pito was sitting on the table beneath the grapevines licking his backside. I see Petra reaching out her hand to stroke his ears. I see Hans pushing open the shutters, opening both wings of the front door and sliding the suitcases across the wooden floor. I see Hanno undoing the clasp of her handbag, taking out a glass vial, unscrewing the top, inverting the vial in the palm of her hand and giving it a shake, then bringing the hand to her mouth and swallowing. I see Messalina coming toward me, placing her hand on my forearm; and I hear her saying: how beautiful. (My bearing is prepossessing both in itself and by the impression it makes, which is the very opposite of that made by Socrates.)

But that isn't why we'd done it either. We hadn't known we would find everything the way we did. We knew Pito would be there, we knew the grapevines would be there, we knew this round, slightly wobbly table would be there, we knew the house would have shutters and double doors, we knew there would be a bit of lawn, we knew there would be a garden hose, a record player and Germaine Montero. We didn't know there would be an inflatable wading pool, we didn't know there would be chest expanders in the garage, we didn't know Georges was going to play a trick on us. But when the cyclist arrived and ate the grapes, our two weeks were already over. What else could we have done? We'd become superfluous. Nothing left to do but pack our bags.

We ought to have known, the way one ought to know everything that comes about just as it was to be expected to, if one has a bit of experience and trusts one's own experience more than one trusts something that one doesn't know but that one thinks needn't come about because it isn't inevitable it do so, but then it does come about, the way a clump of grapes unexpectedly ripens overnight after one has said: this one isn't going to ripen yet, see that yellow bunch over there with the fat grapes on it, but then all at once it's the first bunch that's ripened when no one was expecting it, and you say: I would never in a million years have expected that.

We knew we would have to feed the cat, we knew we would have to water the grapevine, we knew we would have to keep putting things under one of the table's three legs, we knew we would have to close the shutters or the double doors at night, we knew we would have to sprinkle the lawn. We didn't know whether we would have to use the inflatable tub to bathe or float boats in, we didn't know whether we would have to use the chest expanders to tone our muscles or strap the picnic things to the top of the car, we didn't know if we were going to have to let the cyclist eat grapes, until Hans said: time to pack up.

Then all at once it hit us. In a sudden flash of insight, we realized we hadn't watered the cat, hadn't fed the table, hadn't put things under the lawn, hadn't sprinkled the double doors, hadn't closed the grapevine, and that nothing other than the grapevine was to blame for our not having watered the cat, nothing other than the cat was to blame for our not having fed the table, nothing other than the table was to blame for our not having put things under the lawn, nothing other than the lawn was to blame for our not having sprinkled the door, and nothing other than the door was to blame for our not having closed the grapevine.

But we ought to have closed the grapevine, for Georges' sake we ought to have not watered it but closed it, we ought to have devoted this fortnight to closing the grapevine, constructing a wall or at least a sturdy wooden fence around it, and we ought to have fastened the grapes to the vines with chains. We could already hear Georges bawling us out in the distance, and we packed our bags. (So many millions put to the sword, and the richest and fairest part of the world turned upside down for the benefit of the pearl and pepper trades.)

But why else?

THE PTOLEMAISTS

We were sitting, and where we sat we sat at the center. We never sat anywhere anything had a beginning or an end, where anything commenced or ceased. We were sitting, we were there, and we disappeared. That was a bit of earth we were sitting on, either a bit of earth or the chairs or the railing at the harbor. We smelled the tar on the ships. We tasted the salt water of the sea. We saw the rigging on the quay. We felt the warm palings of the gate. We heard the seagulls shrieking and the sirens wailing. Everything with a beginning commenced and was there. Everything with an end ceased and disappeared. We were there, and we were sitting, and once we'd sat, we disappeared.

We were sitting, and where we sat there were things all around us. They had beginning and end. They commenced and ceased. They were there and disappeared. They were finite things that had a beginning, commenced and were there. Finite things that had an end, ceased and disappeared. They had beginning and end. They commenced and ceased. They were there and disappeared. Suddenly the smell of tar entered our nostrils, we smelled it for a while, then we'd had a noseful. The taste of salt water appeared on our lips, we tasted it with our tongues, then we were up to our necks in it. We let our eyes meander about the quay, there were thick cables stretching from all the poles across to the ships, then our eyes were overflowing with the sight of them. We sat among these things, and they gave us a singular pleasure.

We smelled what there was to smell. We tasted what there was to taste. We saw what there was to see. We felt what there was to feel. We heard what there was to hear. We perceived things and gave them their names. They were called tar and ships, salt water and sea, ropes and quay, palings and gate, seagulls and sirens. Things that had no beginning and end, that did not commence and cease, that were not there and did not disappear did not exist, since we perceived these things and they were finite.

Finally these things had become finite for us who were sitting there, since we wished to take our time perceiving things and enjoying them. It was summer, and the finite things were, at this moment, as finite as things possibly can be. We were sitting, and when something happened it happened beneath a finite sky, before a finite sea, upon a finite sand. When we smelled the tar of the ships, when we tasted the salt water of the sea, when we saw the ropes on the quay, when we felt the warm palings of the gate, when we heard the seagulls shrieking and the sirens wailing, all this took place beneath a sky that was finite, before a sea that was finite, upon a sand that was finite.

The sand reached from horizon to horizon. It did not reach beyond it. The sea reached from horizon to horizon. It did not reach beyond it. It was a finite sea. The sky reached from horizon to horizon. It did not reach beyond it. It was a finite sky. It was cloudless and blue. The sky reached from the border of the sand to the border of the sea. The sea reached from the border of the sky to the border of the sand. The sand reached from the border of the sea to the border of the sky. They had beginning and end. They commenced and ceased. They were finite things, and we sat and enjoyed them.

The sun rose, it described its arc, and it set. It rose at the point where sand and sky bordered one another, it described its arc across the finite sky, and it set at the point where sky and sea bordered one another. It was a finite sun that rose, was there and disappeared again. It rose as we were smelling the tar of the ships, it was there as we were tasting the salt water of the sea, as we were seeing the ropes on the quay, as we were feeling the warm palings of the gate, and it set as we were hearing the seagulls shriek and the sirens wail. It shone on all these things we were enjoying, and we enjoyed the things because they were finite and wished for nothing more.

These were finite days which commenced when the sun rose and ceased when the sun set. The sky, which reached from the border of the sand to the border of the sea, the sea, which reached from the border of the sky to the border of the sand, the sand, which reached from the border of the sea to the border of the sky, were as finite as the arc of the sun that created borders for the days. The days had beginning and end. They commenced and ceased. They were there and disappeared. One day after the other commenced and ceased. One day after the other was there and disappeared.

Still these were days that were finite, days that were given borders by nights, when the arc of the sun did not reach across the sky, from the point where sand and sky bordered one another to the point where sky and sea bordered one another. Still these were finite days. Still we were enjoying the finite things we perceived during these finite days. Once more we smelled the tar of the ships, once more we tasted the salt water of the sea, once more we saw the ropes on the quay, once more we felt the warm palings of the gate, once more we heard the shrieks of the seagulls and the wail of the sirens. Still all these things were a singular pleasure beneath the sun. Still the sun was there. Still it was summer.

Was it   it was   it was
        still summer? Still summer   Summer   still
Was it   it was   it was
        summer still? Summer still   Still   summer
        still   Still   still
Was it   summer?   summer it was Summer it was
                  still?   still   Still
Was it summer   Summer   it was   it was summer
              summer?   summer   Summer
Was it still   Still   it was   it was still
        summer   Summer   Summer
Was it   still?   still it was Still   it was

THE LAST BOTTLE

So as to have something, I said.

What do you mean, said Hanno.

More something on the inside, said Messalina.

You can't be serious, said Hans.

Me too, Petra said.

I said: we are taking something with us though.

Hanno said: I don't get it.

Messalina said: he means something on the inside.

Hans said: that would be news to me.

Petra said: me too.

Not like that, I said, but after all something.

Does anyone understand this, said Hanno, because I don't.

Let's have another round, Messalina said, maybe it'll be something on the inside after all.

So what aren't we going to take with us, said Hans, if we take it with us.

Some of the red, said Petra, if we take some of the white.

You've had quite enough, Hanno said.

Have another one, said Hans, maybe it will help.

That was plenty for me, I said.

Montaigne said: the profit of wealth lies in one's having enough when one doesn't wish for more.

Well, but that depends, Hans said, because if the profit of wealth lies in one's having enough, then one has enough when one wants to have more. That's my opinion.

Bottoms up, Messalina said, it's almost time.

Just a minute, I said, but if the profit of wealth doesn't lie in one's having enough, *then* one has enough when one wants to have *more*

and if the profit of wealth lies in one's *not* having enough, then one has enough when one wants to have more,

and if the profit of wealth lies in one's having enough, then one does *not* have enough when one wants to have *more,*

and if the profit of wealth lies in one's having *enough,* then one has enough when one does *not* want to have more.

Not so fast, Hans said, because it isn't so simple.

That's plenty, Hanno said, you're both stewed to the gills.

The matter hasn't been settled yet, said Hans,

because if the profit of wealth does *not* lie in one's *not* having enough, then one has enough when one wants to have more,

and if the profit of wealth does *not* lie in one's having enough, then one does *not* have enough when one wants to have more,

and if the profit of wealth does *not* lie in one's having enough, then one has enough when one does *not* want to have more,

and if the profit of wealth lies in one's *not* having enough, then one does *not* have enough when one wants to have more,

and if the profit of wealth lies in one's *not* having enough, then one has enough when one does *not* want to have more,

and if the profit of wealth lies in one's having enough, then one does *not* have enough when one does *not* want to have more.

Now I've really had enough, I said,

since if the profit of wealth does *not* lie in one's *not* having enough, then one does *not* have enough when one wants to have more,

and if the profit of wealth does *not* lie in one's *not* having enough, then one has enough when one does *not* want to have more,

and if the profit of wealth does *not* lie in one's having enough, then one does *not* have enough when one does *not* want to have more,

and if the profit of wealth lies in one's *not* having enough, then one does *not* have enough when one does *not* want to have more.

Come on, we'll meet you out front, said Messalina.

Just wait a sec, said Hans, we're finished.

When the two of you get started, Hanno said.

We're finished, I said.

You look it, said Messalina.

Just one last question, Hans said.

We've got to hit the road, Hanno said.

I said: is there anything left?

OK, said Hans, listen to this: if the profit of wealth were not to lie in one's not wanting to have more, then one still wouldn't have enough when one didn't want to have more, right?

We'll have to work it out, I said.

So you're not going to take anything with you after all, Hanno said.

The last bottle, said Messalina.

But that's the end, said Hans.

Me too, Petra said.

STREETS

Sihdi, said Hans, keep your right side free, because you can do what you want if you have to leave this city and you don't want to leave because you want to remain in it, but all the same you have to leave because you cannot remain, but without being able to find your way out on streets whose names do not remind you of names you want to forget because you want not to remember them, but all the same you cannot help remembering them because they are names you've heard so often, names you wanted not to hear, because you'd heard them so often and because every time you heard them they recalled to you events you wanted nothing to do with and didn't want to hear about because fathers had told tales of them, and not only because the telling of these tales summoned up the names you'd heard and didn't want to hear, but because fathers had told tales of them out of reverence for names and out of pride over events, and we didn't want to hear anything about reverence for names and pride over events, but all the same we had to find our way out of this network of streets with names that reminded fathers of names we wanted to forget because it's only reverence and pride that summon up these names.

Sihdi, are you free on the right? said Hans. Let's pay no attention, I said, because you can do what you want if you have to leave this city and you don't want to leave because you want to remain

99

in it, but all the same you have to leave because you cannot remain, and the way out cannot be found without crossing this network of streets with these names that remind fathers of names you want to forget because it's only reverence and pride that summon up these names and because it makes no difference at all which streets you take because all the names remind us of events about which fathers told tales out of reverence and pride.

How are things looking on your right? said Hans, because we had to leave this city and because it makes no difference whether you take the cours de l'Argonne, which leads to the place de la Victoire, or whether you take the cours de la Somme, which leads to the place de la Victoire, or whether you take the cours de l'Yser, which intersects the cours de la Marne, which leads to the place de la Victoire and from there to the cours de la Libération, and because you are forced to hear names that remind you of events fathers speak of with pride and reverence, you hear the names and remember the events which you cannot remember because you weren't there when they happened and you've only heard about them from fathers and you wonder why you ought to remember them, because the names are there to make you remember them and you don't understand that you ought to remember them because these are events that remind you of nothing but reverence and pride and you don't know what these things are.

Sihdi, watch your right, said Hans, but because we are forced to hear names that remind us of events which are events that bring to mind nothing but reverence and pride, and we don't know what these things are because they have become obscure, although we do know these events ought to bring to mind not only these now obscure feelings but also horror and shame, we remember them in other ways, because the ones who give out the names are not thinking of horror and shame and don't wish to call these things to mind by the names they give out, because they understand that names which call to mind horror and shame do a disservice to the cause they are intending to serve when they give out the names that call to mind events which, they believe, ought to summon up reverence and pride and not horror and shame.

Your right, Sihdi, said Hans, you've really got to keep it free, because the ones who give the streets their names are not thinking of horror and shame and are not intending to call these things to mind when they give the streets their names, because they don't want to do a disservice to what they believe is suggested by reverence and pride, and want to profit from something that was once horror and shame, while they want to call up feelings that no longer exist because they have become obscure out of horror and shame, which, however, they refuse to accept, because they want to profit from reverence and pride, which have no place in horror and shame.

So how's it coming, Sihdi, Hans said, are you keeping your right side free? But since you can do what you want if you have to leave this city and aren't ready to accept that it is horror and shame that make a human being human rather than reverence and pride, but rather that someone exists who can say these things, horror and shame and reverence and pride, and that you can find the one who can say what is meant when one says horror and pain and reverence and pride, and that you can find the one who can say what names are and that he is a human being who says horror and shame and reverence and pride, because you can do what you want, you'll still keep meeting the person who summons up names out of pride and events out of reverence, who is said to be more human than human because he can remember names and events that call to mind horror and shame, and so you keep going in a circle and your right side isn't free.

BIOGRAPHICAL NOTE

Ludwig Harig, born in 1927 in Sulzbach/Saarland, worked as a teacher before becoming a free-lance writer in 1974. In the 1950s he was part of the experimental "Stuttgart School" around Max Bense, which sought to develop narrative techniques that would free language from the ballast of fixed signification. The 1960s saw him branching out into different genres, in particular the radio play, and by the late 1970s he had developed the self-reflexive, playful, but realistic chronicler's style that characterizes his late work. He is best known for his autobiographical trilogy: *Ordnung ist das ganze Leben* (1986), *Weh dem, der aus der Reihe tanzt* (1990), and *Wer mit den Wölfen heult wird Wolf* (1996).

Other works by Harig include:
Sprechstunden für die deutsch-französische Verständigung und die Mitglieder des Gemeinsamen Marktes: ein Familienroman, 1971
Allseitige Beschreibung der Welt, 1974
Rousseau: Der Roman vom Ursprung der Natur im Gehirn, 1978
Heimweh, 1979
Der kleine Brixius, 1980
Heilige Kühe der Deutschen, 1981
Die Hortensien der Frau Roselius, 1992

Susan Bernofsky has translated works by Robert Walser, Gregor von Rezzori, Peter Szondi, Yoko Tawada, and is currently at work on a book of stories by Jenny Erpenbeck. She teaches at Bard College.